MERGER CONSULTING: What makes it different?
Michael Groh, consultant

1) Mutual respect and good chemistry is essential between the executive directors of each organization considering merger (or, if lucky, there is an ED vacancy at one organization)

2) Mission and philosophy of the organizations must be compatible - as values and beliefs cannot be merged.

3) Organizational cultures must have good potential for fitting together, otherwise a merged single structure will have two cultures for a long and likely awkward time.

4) Different merger models (and their pros and cons) must be understood and communicated - so as to get the best fit. The "Jonah and the whale" mental model is often predominant.
("open window" allows consideration of imaginative others)

5) The "M" word (merger) tends to produce backlash, around loss of identity and a felt devaluing of hard work done; and, from staff, on "me" issues – especially if it's a "shotgun merger."
(affiliation/partnering language is often better used early).

6) Full disclosure of information, especially information difficult to disclose, builds trust early. Failure to do so or reluctance / "half - disclosing " erodes trust: "What aren't they telling us?"

7) Third party mediation dynamics and the role of the mediator provides a facilitator model for the consultant. Know third party mediation philosophy, strategies and interventions.

8) Almost certainly a feasibility/investigation phase Is needed - with the desired result being a thoughtful and well grounded decision about whether to continue to plan for merger.
(a credible, balanced feasibility group needs to be created and empowered to go through this phase)

9) Pace and passions change, creating shifting and often de-motivating "hot and cold," "too fast - too slow" dynamics.

The Nonprofit Mergers Workbook

The Leader's Guide to Considering, Negotiating, and Executing a Merger

David La Piana

AMHERST H.
WILDER
FOUNDATION

SAINT PAUL,
MINNESOTA

We thank The David and Lucile Packard Foundation and the
Amherst H. Wilder Foundation for supporting the production of this publication.

Published by the Amherst H. Wilder Foundation
Copyright © 2000 David La Piana

The Amherst H. Wilder Foundation is one of the largest and
oldest endowed human service and community development
organizations in America. For more than ninety years, the
Wilder Foundation has been providing health and human services that help children and families grow strong, the elderly
age with dignity, and the community grow in its ability to meet
its own needs.

We hope you find this book helpful! Should you need additional
information about our services, please contact: Services to
Organizations, Amherst H. Wilder Foundation, 919 Lafond
Avenue, Saint Paul, MN 55104, phone (651) 642-4022.

For information about other Wilder Foundation publications,
please see the order form on the last page or contact:

Publishing Center
Amherst H. Wilder Foundation
919 Lafond Avenue
Saint Paul, MN 55104

1-800-274-6024
www.wilder.org

Edited by Vincent Hyman
Design and cover illustration by Rebecca Andrews

Manufactured in the United States of America

First printing, July 2000

Library of Congress Cataloging-in-Publication Data

La Piana, David
    The nonprofit mergers workbook / David La Piana.
        p. cm.
    Includes bibliographical references and index.
    ISBN 0-940069-21-0
      1. Consolidation and merger of corporations. 2. Nonprofit
Organizations. I. Title.

HF2746.2.L33 2000
658.1'6--dc21   00-030504

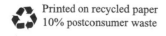

This book is dedicated to my parents, Charles and Virginia La Piana.

Acknowledgments

The author wishes to acknowledge his debt to the following persons and organizations, without whose support this project would not have been possible. Heather Gowdy of La Piana Associates, Inc. provided invaluable editorial assistance, preparation of worksheets, and writing of case studies; she redrafted sections of the workbook and contributed innumerable suggestions for its improvement. Alfredo Vergara-Lobo of La Piana Associates, Inc. carefully read the text, drafted the case studies, and annotated the references. Mike Allison, Steve Lew, and Tim Wolfred of CompassPoint, our partners in the AIDS Service Organizations Strategic Restructuring Project, helped test and revise the costs section of the workbook. The members of the Strategic Solutions Project's Advisory Board—James E. Canales and Martha Campbell of The James Irvine Foundation, Barbara Kibbe and Richard Green of The David and Lucile Packard Foundation, and Steve Toben and Natasha Terk of The William and Flora Hewlett Foundation—provided moral, intellectual, and financial support for this project.

A special thanks to those people who reviewed the field test draft of this book:

Mike Allison	Michael Groh	Christine Park
Jane Arsenault	Robert Harrington	Karen Ray
Daniel Bowling	Norah Holmgren	Arthur Rieman
Martha Campbell	Ginger Hope	William P. Ryan
Tom Courtney	Linda Hoskins	Robert Teeter
Liza Culick	Bob Kardon	Jim Thomas
Claudia Dengler	Amelia Kohm	Janice Williams
Kate Dewey	Carol Lukas	Linda Williams
Margaret Donohoe	Tom McLaughlin	David Yamakawa Jr.
Elizabeth Elliott	Richard L. Moyers	

Preface

I first became interested in nonprofit mergers when, as executive director of a growing human service nonprofit in the early 1990s, I led my organization through three mergers in the space of four years. Each merger experience was truly unique and entirely different from the others. I now refer to these early experiences as "the good, the bad, and the ugly." Despite their pronounced differences, I found certain common themes in these experiences. This paradox intrigued me. Struggling to make sense of these mergers, I was surprised to discover that I could find no resources to turn to: no books, articles, or pamphlets on the topic; no other executive directors who had been through a merger whom I could identify and question. I was alone.

Motivated in part by a desire to better understand my own merger experiences, in part by a need to find others who had similar experiences, and also in part by my realization that the field was lacking in resources on this important activity, I wrote a short article describing my ideas about nonprofit mergers for *The Nonprofit Times*. Shortly thereafter I had the good fortune to meet Nancy Axelrod, founding president of the National Center for Nonprofit Boards. Nancy and I agreed that a monograph on the topic was necessary, and that I would write it.

Appearing in 1994, *Nonprofit Mergers: The Board's Responsibility to Consider the Unthinkable*[1] was the first widely published attempt at describing this increasingly prominent type of partnership. Since that date a trickle of publications and case studies has emerged. (See Resource List, pages 173–178, for a list of these.) The eager reception given to these works by the nonprofit community attests to the sustained and indeed growing level of interest in this topic among managers, board members, funders, and consultants.

I next explored the features of collaboration and strategic restructuring in a 1997 monograph, *Beyond Collaboration: Strategic Restructuring of Nonprofit Organizations*. This project was conceived, initiated, and supported by The James Irvine Foundation, a California philanthropy that had recently identified merger activity

---

[1] Available from the National Center for Nonprofit Boards, Washington, D.C.

as an important new area of endeavor and concern for nonprofits and funders alike. In 1998, after the initial run of 10,000 was exhausted, *Beyond Collaboration* was reissued in a revised edition. This work coined the phrase *strategic restructuring* as shorthand for the full range of nonprofit partnership options: mergers, asset transfers, joint ventures, administrative or back office consolidations, joint programming, fiscal sponsorship arrangements, confederations, provider networks, parent-subsidiary relationships, and virtual organizations. While this term is gaining currency, these partnership options are still often referred to as "strategic alliances," or as "mergers and strategic alliances." The latter phrase is more technically accurate (mergers are a more intense form of partnership than alliances), but highlights the need for a single term to cover the continuum.

Whatever they are called, these endeavors have in common a single, crucial factor that distinguishes them from the broader concept of collaboration. In strategic restructuring, there is a change in the locus of control of at least a part of one or more of the organizations involved. This simple, central fact leads to most of the complications encountered in strategic restructuring, and in particular to the emotional roller-coaster ride that characterizes a nonprofit merger.

In 1997, at the urging of the James Irvine Foundation, the David and Lucile Packard Foundation, and the William and Flora Hewlett Foundation, I founded La Piana Associates, Inc., a consulting firm that helps nonprofits and foundations manage strategic issues. These foundations have made multiyear commitments to support The Strategic Solutions Project, an effort to expand the knowledge and practice base of the nonprofit sector with regard to strategic restructuring. Strategic Solutions has an ongoing research agenda and intends to produce materials (such as this workbook) of use to nonprofit leaders, board members, funders, and consultants. The project also provides training programs for nonprofit leaders and consultants and is actively seeking new and innovative forms of strategic restructuring.

The vast majority of La Piana Associates, Inc.'s work involves mergers or other forms of strategic restructuring. Since 1997, we've given dozens of workshops and speeches around the country to national and regional gatherings of funders, associations of nonprofit managers, and meetings of nonprofit management consultants. We have also facilitated and studied a number of strategic restructuring efforts, particularly mergers. At last count our total merger experience was sixty projects.

One theme, almost a plea, has emerged again and again in these interactions: the need for clear, practical, usable information that is accessible to nonprofit managers and their board members as they consider merger, the most common form of strategic restructuring. With no signs that the current trend toward partnering will abate, this workbook is intended to help nonprofit leaders engaged in or considering a merger to make the best decisions for their organizations, their fields, and their communities.

MEMO

TO:

Bryan Barry	Judy Sharken Simon
Mary Ann Hennen	Debi Krause
Ceil Mead	Yorn Yan
Carol Zapfel	Carol Lukas
Kate Murphy	Sue Saunders
Jack Fortin	Lesley Blicker
Emil Angelica	Barb Rose
Jody Swenson	Jim Tyree
Linda Hoskins	Patti Jo Martain
Maricarmen Cortes	

FROM: Kirsten Nielsen, Publishing Assistant

DATE: July 17, 2000

I am happy to present a copy of the latest book from the Publishing Center, *The Nonprofit Mergers Workbook: The Leader's Guide to Considering, Negotiating, and Executing a Merger*, by David La Piana.

Please let us know of anyone who might be interested in this publication. We'd be happy to send them our catalog.

Contents

Introduction

WHEREVER I have traveled, nonprofit leaders generally agree that the sector is witnessing a dramatic increase in the frequency with which mergers are being considered and executed.[2] The variety, comprehensiveness, and quality of available materials on the topic is growing; conference agendas and the contents of sector periodicals increasingly include related subject matter. Foundations, which fund much of the research and development in the nonprofit sector, are funding mergers and other forms of strategic restructuring, both directly and through the development of knowledge about the practice.

Hostile takeover, acquisition, layoffs, and similar terms are frequently used (often inappropriately) to describe the experience or results of nonprofit mergers. Mergers are perplexing, confusing, frustrating, and often downright frightening. Why are nonprofit leaders so keenly interested in a topic with such negative connotations?

The consensus among people studying mergers seems to be that economic conditions are driving the sector toward a shake-out and consolidation. I agree with this contention, but I feel it describes only one of several motivators for mergers. This workbook will look at a variety of economic and other factors that I believe are at play. These factors include the growth of the nonprofit sector, competition with businesses and other nonprofits, devolution, welfare reform, upward pressure on salaries, and the realization by a growing number of nonprofit managers that mergers are viable options when until recently they would not have been considered.

---

[2] Statistical evidence on the actual number of nonprofit mergers is lacking due to the way the Internal Revenue Service and the states record such transactions as merger and dissolution.

Growth and competition

The unparalleled growth of the nonprofit sector was spearheaded by the expansion of the health and human services subsector, which began with the War on Poverty and Great Society programs of the 1960s. The continuing growth of the sector has led to well over one million non-religious nonprofit organizations in the United States. More than thirty thousand new nonprofits are created each year, according to the Internal Revenue Service. This growth has increased competition for funding. Despite the dramatic and steady rise in assets experienced by many foundations during the latter half of the 1990s (due to both a bullish stock market and numerous health care conversions), available grant funds have not kept up with the needs of an ever-growing number of organizations attempting to address increasingly complex issues.

Compounding this competition for donor dollars is the entrance of businesses into territory traditionally held by nonprofits. Drug treatment, vocational rehabilitation, primary health care, hospitals, schools, the arts, housing, and social services have all experienced the entrance of these new, often sophisticated and well-capitalized, competitors. These players have changed the rules of the game. They bring techniques such as front-end capital investment in better facilities, organized efforts at increasing customer responsiveness, expensive marketing campaigns, and sophisticated systems for cost projection and control. Some of these techniques are foreign to nonprofits, and can leave them playing catch-up, or in some cases, not playing at all. The growing competition between businesses and nonprofits has increased competitiveness among nonprofits themselves.

Devolution and welfare reform

Devolution is another driver of the trend toward strategic restructuring, specifically in the human services. The federal government is turning over to the states the responsibility to provide (and pay for) benefits and services for the poor. In turn, many states have pushed the responsibility to local jurisdictions. Welfare reform is also beginning to impact the aims of the traditional human services sector, which grew up over the past thirty-five years as an adjunct to a permanent welfare state. An unstated but essential fact is that ending poverty was never an explicit goal of the human services subsector. Instead, this subsector's purpose has usually been expressed as alleviating human suffering. Now that welfare reform is attempting to remove permanency from the welfare system, nonprofits face new challenges devising ways to quickly move their clients into self-sufficiency.

Salary pressure

Another motivation for strategic restructuring is salary pressure. Baby boomers have risen to the leadership ranks of many nonprofits, putting upward pressure on salaries. With children to educate and mortgages to meet, they seek better compensation each year. At the younger end of the spectrum, entry-level positions are now being filled by employees who grew up in the less idealistic and less financially secure 1980s; they expect and need to earn a living wage. Finally, the growth of nonprofit management education programs has professionalized management, bringing better skills and heightened expectations around compensation.

These economic pressures are not going to disappear. Rather, they will make it more difficult for nonprofits to rely on a favorite economic strategy: expecting employees to subsidize the organization's mission through acceptance of discounted wages and minimal fringe benefits.

Merger as an option

In addition to the harsh realities of nonprofit economics, the success of an increasing number of mergers is inspiring other nonprofit leaders to take a closer look at this strategy. Though these leaders may have previously considered a merger but abandoned the idea as too risky, they now feel more comfortable going where others have gone before—especially if those others live to tell about it.

One unfortunate result of all the economic pressures the sector faces is a tendency to shift the organization's focus from mission to economic survival. The social mission—the reason most people came into the sector in the first place (it certainly wasn't to get rich!)—seems to get lost in the press of financial crises and concerns.

Over time this loss of mission focus becomes increasingly painful to nonprofit leaders. In a recent survey conducted by The Support Center for Nonprofit Management/Nonprofit Development Center in San Francisco, 137 executive directors were asked how long they had been in their jobs, if they wanted their next job to be as an executive director, and what their predecessors went on to do. The results of this poll were quite remarkable. Two-thirds of those surveyed were in their first executive director job, and only one-fourth said that they would seek another nonprofit executive director position. When asked what their immediate predecessors had gone on to do after leaving the executive director position, only 14 percent reported that that person had gone on to another executive director position. Low pay and stress are obvious contributing factors to this situation.[3]

Stress and burnout are heightened by the inability of many nonprofit leaders, despite often superhuman efforts, to effectively advance their organizations' missions. Often these executive directors are competent and diligent leaders. Nonetheless, when the press of economic survival overtakes the earnest desire to accomplish a mission, the job may cease to be satisfying.

---

[3] *Leadership Lost: Report on an ED Tenure Study* by Tim Wolfred, The Support Center for Nonprofit Management, 1999.

Why Merger?

Heightened economic pressures, greater competition, new opportunities, a desperate desire to refocus on mission, basic changes in the paradigm of human service delivery, decreased arts funding, workplace giving (you choose), are all challenges that push nonprofit managers to consider new and different solutions to their problems. "We can't go on long like this," is a frequent lament.

This is clear enough, but the question remains, why merger? What does this solution offer? The participants in a merger often hope for benefits that are immediate and quantifiable:

> We need to squeeze an extra twenty thousand dollars out of next year's budget. Maybe a merger will do that.

> If we go from two executive directors to one, we'll save enough to hire an additional social worker and to pay the rent increase.

Unfortunately, immediate savings are seldom the case in a merger. Chapter 7, Funding a Merger, describes the costs of a merger transaction. These can be substantial. While grant assistance may be available, and costs can be controlled through a variety of techniques described in that chapter, two facts remain:

1) Money will be spent to create your partnership—lawyers, consultants, printing, moving, and other one-time costs can add up.

2) Any savings realized by consolidating the executive director positions and other administrative positions will probably go quickly to meet another need—to augment or create a development department, to underwrite a sorely-needed chief financial officer position, to grant salary increases that level the playing field between organizations, or to buy new equipment.

There is no question that these are important things on which to spend money, and that they can add value to the merged organization, but in making these choices, you have not actually *lowered* operating costs, and you have not in the end saved money.

The real benefits of merger are not short-term and tactical but medium- to long-term and strategic:

- Better market positioning
- A larger market share
- A higher public profile
- Greater political influence
- More strategic fundraising
- A larger staff, allowing greater specialization of functions and the provision of more service
- The creation of a continuum of services under unified control
- Better economies of scale

These are the likely, and substantial, benefits of a merger, but they take time, planning, and funding to realize.

A merger should be considered when

- The level of integration and synergy sought by the potential partners cannot be achieved through lesser means.
- Clients and the community already think of the potential partners as the same organization, repeatedly confusing their identities.
- A larger entity is needed to compete with other large nonprofits or businesses.
- The organization has lost steam, experienced a scandal, or for other reasons cannot sustain and renew itself.

Mergers are powerful tools that should be applied judiciously. A merger should never be acquiesced to solely because a major funder is demanding it, executive directors have arranged it (along with their future roles in the merged organization), or the board chairs, old friends, discussed it among themselves and thought it a great idea.

The real benefits of merger are not short-term and tactical but medium- to long-term and strategic

When properly conceived and implemented, however, a merger can strengthen your organization by allowing you to benefit from your partner's experience, resources, and skills. This is most often a two-way street, with your organization also contributing experience, resources, and skills to the mix. Look to the potential whole. Is it greater than the sum of the two separate organizational parts? If so, merger might be the right option for your organization.

Other Partnership Options

While this book focuses on mergers, other partnership options yield some of the same benefits as a merger, while preserving a greater degree of independence. These options should be reviewed before a merger is decided upon. La Piana Associates, Inc. developed The Partnership Matrix (Figure 1, page 6) to help our clients understand the range of strategic restructuring and collaboration options available. These options lie in a field defined by both a horizontal axis and a vertical axis. Generally, as you move toward the right along the horizontal axis, you experience a higher level of integration and a corresponding lessening of autonomy. The vertical axis represents the degree to which a partnership focuses on programmatic issues (the direct services that an organization provides); administration (the office and management functions that support operations); or a combination of both.

The following definitions describe the options shown in The Partnership Matrix.

Figure 1. The Partnership Matrix

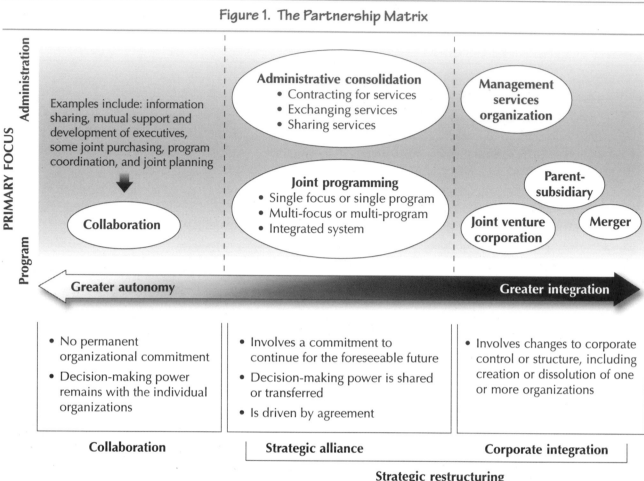

Collaboration

A relationship whereby two or more organizations confer, share information, or work together toward some mutual benefit while maintaining separate organizations, distributed decision-making power, and organizational autonomy. Such relationships typically do not involve a permanent organizational commitment.

Strategic restructuring

An ongoing relationship involving two or more organizations established to increase administrative efficiency or further the programmatic ends and social mission of one or more of the participating organizations through shared, transferred, or combined services, resources, or programs. Strategic restructuring always involves a partial or total change in the locus of control of one or more of the partnering organizations.

Strategic alliance

A strategic restructuring that involves a commitment to continue, for the foreseeable future, shared or transferred decision-making power, and some type of formal agreement.

Administrative consolidation

A strategic restructuring that involves the sharing, exchanging, or contracting of administrative functions to increase the administrative efficiency of one or more of the organizations. There is no change to the corporate structure of any of the organizations involved.

Joint programming

A strategic restructuring that involves the joint launching and managing of one or more programs to further the programmatic mission of the participating organizations. There is no change to the corporate structure of any of the organizations involved.

Corporate integration

A strategic restructuring that involves changes to corporate control or structure, including the creation or dissolution of one or more organizations.

Management service organization

A strategic restructuring that involves the creation of a new organization in order to integrate administrative functions and increase the administrative efficiency of the participating organizations.

Joint venture corporation

A strategic restructuring that involves the creation of a new organization to further a specific administrative or programmatic end of two or more organizations. Partner organizations share governance of the new organization.

Parent-subsidiary

A strategic restructuring that involves the integration of some administrative functions and programmatic services to increase the administrative efficiency and program quality of one or more organizations through the creation of a new organization or designation of a preexisting organization to oversee the administrative functions and programmatic services of one or more other organizations.

Merger

A strategic restructuring that involves the integration of all programmatic and administrative functions to increase administrative efficiency and program quality of one or more organizations through the dissolution of one or more organizations or the creation of a new merged organization.

The Decision Tree below, when used in conjunction with The Partnership Matrix on page 6, will help you determine which form of partnership is right for your organization. Work through the Decision Tree with a group of informed leaders from your organization.

Decision Tree 1. What Form of Strategic Restructuring is Right for Us?

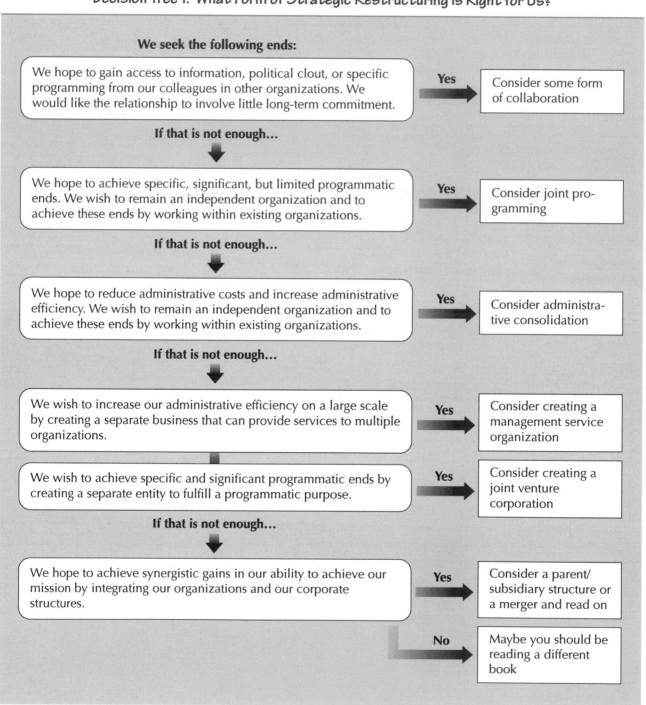

We seek the following ends:

We hope to gain access to information, political clout, or specific programming from our colleagues in other organizations. We would like the relationship to involve little long-term commitment. → **Yes** → Consider some form of collaboration

If that is not enough...

We hope to achieve specific, significant, but limited programmatic ends. We wish to remain an independent organization and to achieve these ends by working within existing organizations. → **Yes** → Consider joint programming

If that is not enough...

We hope to reduce administrative costs and increase administrative efficiency. We wish to remain an independent organization and to achieve these ends by working within existing organizations. → **Yes** → Consider administrative consolidation

If that is not enough...

We wish to increase our administrative efficiency on a large scale by creating a separate business that can provide services to multiple organizations. → **Yes** → Consider creating a management service organization

We wish to achieve specific and significant programmatic ends by creating a separate entity to fulfill a programmatic purpose. → **Yes** → Consider creating a joint venture corporation

If that is not enough...

We hope to achieve synergistic gains in our ability to achieve our mission by integrating our organizations and our corporate structures. → **Yes** → Consider a parent/subsidiary structure or a merger and read on

→ **No** → Maybe you should be reading a different book

How to Use This Book

This workbook takes you through the steps involved in considering, negotiating, and executing a merger. Details of structural options, negotiation techniques, and the costs associated with such efforts are described, and worksheets and Decision Trees guide you through the maze of options. Some information on implementation is provided to help you get started on the long road to integrating systems and staff after merger. In-depth implementation is a critical topic that draws heavily from fields as diverse as organizational development, financial management, information technology, and human resource management. It is deserving of a book unto itself and is beyond the scope of this work.

The consideration and negotiation of a merger has much in common with other forms of strategic restructuring. However, the level of integration involved in a nonprofit merger raises the stakes and consequently the anxiety level of everyone involved to a degree usually not felt in other forms of strategic restructuring. Therefore, while this workbook will be of use to partnering efforts of all kinds, it focuses especially on the needs of merger-makers.

We recommend that a team comprised of both board members and senior managers complete the workbook process together, pooling their input and ideas and working to form one opinion on the best course of action. If an organization is considering the possibility of a merger, but is not in the thick of an actual merger negotiation with another nonprofit, this workbook will help leaders sort out their organization's position relative to a merger. It will also alert them to the myriad issues they will face if they decide to move forward, identify a partner, and try to strike a deal.

If, on the other hand, two[4] nonprofits have already come together in an effort to determine if a merger is the right strategic choice, this workbook should be used jointly. Often the worksheets can be completed by each partner separately and shared along the way. For example, Worksheet 2, Desired Outcomes, on page 183, helps a nonprofit to identify its desired outcomes from a merger. Make extra copies so that each party can complete the worksheet and share its answers with the other party. In this way the workbook will help the negotiators move step-by-step through the process.

If a consultant is engaged to facilitate negotiations, this workbook will serve as a useful tool for him or her. This is especially important at present since the frequency of nonprofit mergers is rising, but as yet, few nonprofit consultants have substantial experience in the area. We have included a special section just for consultants (Chapter 8, For Consultants Only, page 141).

In whatever context the workbook is used, feel free to skip some of the sections and worksheets, focusing on those that fit the immediate issues facing your organization. This workbook is not a blueprint that must be copied and followed to the

---

[4] Throughout the workbook we use the example of two merging organizations. However, mergers occasionally involve three or more parties. We think readers will find the processes recommended herein equally useful, regardless of the number of organizations involved.

letter. It is, rather, a resource into which you should dip as often as is necessary and helpful. Some readers might not use a particular section of the workbook at first. However, when problems arise in the area covered by that section, our guidelines and advice might help. Other readers might not use any of the worksheets as tools per se, but will read the text and worksheets for guidance.

The overall process I recommend, and the process portrayed in this workbook, is as follows:

Chapter 1   Forms of Merger
What are the options for structuring your merger?

This chapter offers an overview of the structural and mechanical options for merger. There are many ways to structure and execute a merger—perhaps more options than you have considered to date.

Chapter 2   Internal Self-Assessment
What makes you a good candidate for a merger?

What factors will enable you to conduct "good-faith" merger negotiations and make you a good partner? What factors should make you think twice about entering into any negotiations, at least right now? Equally important from the outset, what do you want from a merger and how will you know whether you have gotten it?

Chapter 3   Interorganizational Assessment
What makes a good partner for your organization?

What do you seek in a merger partner? What attributes, skills, or assets are you looking for? Whom do you know? What is your organization's history with a specific merger candidate? How do you first broach the subject of merger with representatives of another organization?

Chapter 4   Anticipating Difficulties and Roadblocks
What are common problems in merger negotiations?

This chapter offers a heads-up about some of the bumps you may encounter along the road to a merger. The good news is that you can usually predict where the rough spots will be.

Chapter 5   Negotiation Stages and Strategies
Is this partnership worth pursuing? If it is, how do you negotiate a merger?

Next you must determine whether enough commonality of interest exists to move you to open negotiations. If so, each organization makes a commitment to enter into good-faith negotiations. The negotiations process that seems to work best is a simple one: identify all the issues to be addressed, categorize them, and begin working through them. This chapter shows you how.

Chapter 6 Implementation
Once the terms of the partnership are agreed upon, how do you make the merger a reality?

> The real work—and benefits—of merger grows from your efforts to integrate systems and create a new culture. This chapter helps you get started.

Chapter 7 Funding a Merger
What is it going to cost? Where will I find the money?

> Mergers cost money. This chapter helps you to calculate the cost of your merger and suggests avenues to pursue for funding.

Chapter 8 For Consultants Only

> This chapter offers advice for consultants embarking on their first merger experience, as well as suggestions for more experienced consultants.

The journey to a nonprofit merger will always be bumpy, but if everyone keeps an eye on the prize—the nonprofit's mission—the destination can be very satisfying

The journey to a nonprofit merger will always be bumpy, but if everyone keeps an eye on the prize—the nonprofit's mission—the destination can be very satisfying.[5]

An important note on legal issues

Please note that I am not a lawyer and this workbook does not offer legal advice. I have tried to indicate places where competent legal counsel is essential. But in general, you should be aware that many actions, ranging from changing bylaws in order to accommodate a "parent" nonprofit, to actually merging organizations, can create legal, liability, and tax issues. Most nonprofits do not need (and in any event, cannot afford) to use an attorney to *negotiate* their mergers, but they do need legal assistance to formalize the merger. It is essential that once you think you know what you want to do, and before you actually do it, you consult an attorney specializing in nonprofit law in your state.

One way to save money and also to avoid the potential for conflict (attorney-to-attorney conflict, that is) is to hire a single attorney jointly with your partner organization. Many attorneys will be reluctant to represent both parties, but you can argue that you are not hiring them to "represent" you, merely to review your proposed merger agreement and point out any red flags before you move forward. In practice, attorneys specializing in nonprofit law are accustomed to these requests—another reason to seek out and use these specialists.

---

[5] For further information or assistance, readers are directed to visit the author's web site at www.lapiana.org.

Introduction to Case Studies

Throughout this workbook I have included numerous anecdotes from mergers La Piana Associates, Inc. has observed or participated in, as well as completed samples of each worksheet. To provide a more complete picture of the merger process, two case studies run throughout the text. At the end of Chapters 2–7, you will find the next segment of each case study. Between the two you should get a good picture of what can happen. The case studies begin below, with introductions to the organizations involved. (Note: these organizations are fictional composites and are not meant to represent any specific organization or situation.)

In a nutshell...

Stop HIV and Contra SIDA

The agencies share a mission focus and have collaborated on special projects in the past. While Stop HIV is well known for its fundraising abilities, Contra SIDA often feels overwhelmed by these tasks. However, both executive directors (Mary and Carmen) are aware of the growing financial challenges facing AIDS-related services and have knowledge of successful mergers in their area. They do some research on mergers, share their ideas, and decide to present their findings to their respective boards.

Stop HIV and Contra SIDA

Stop HIV is a $3.3 million agency dedicated to the eradication of HIV infection. Located in a major western city, Stop HIV runs citywide programs on HIV education and prevention, neighborhood empowerment through healthier lifestyles, and a 24-hour, award-winning hot line for teens and their families. Stop HIV provides most of its services in neighborhoods throughout the city, and serves mostly English-speaking residents of various ages and backgrounds. The board of Stop HIV is very involved in fundraising. In fact, it is a board duty that is taken very seriously by the organization, and Stop HIV is known throughout the city for its fundraising skills. As Stop HIV's executive director Mary Martin put it, "we may not have the best mix of board members in terms of socioeconomic diversity, but we have an excellent fundraising team. If they'll raise funds for us, we'll recruit them." As the founding executive director, Mary has been with Stop HIV for eleven years.

Contra SIDA (Spanish for "Against AIDS") is a $2.9 million agency dedicated to decreasing the current rate of HIV infection and AIDS-related deaths in the Latino community. Contra SIDA operates unique HIV education, prevention, counseling, and therapy programs for bilingual and monolingual Latinos. Most of Contra SIDA's services are provided on site at their offices in the heart of the Latino barrio. Contra SIDA is the only agency in the city where this level of mental health services is available to Spanish-speaking individuals and families. While hardworking and proud of the services they provide, the seven board members at Contra SIDA often feel overwhelmed by dwindling funds and increased competition. When asked to describe her board, Contra SIDA's executive director Carmen Contreras responded: "While we work well together and are accomplishing a lot, we also have a hard time recruiting members and raising funds, and this can be disconcerting at times." Carmen has been Contra SIDA's executive director for eighteen months, and is the second executive director in Contra SIDA's six years of operation.

During her tenure as executive director at Stop HIV, Mary has seen both abundance and scarcity with regard to the funding available for AIDS-related services. However, recent changes in the AIDS epidemic, coupled with unexpected policy changes, seem to be making it harder than ever to gain funding for AIDS-service organizations. Carmen is also concerned about the shrinking pool of money, having just lost a large chunk of funding for psychotherapy services at Contra SIDA, and she wonders how this loss will affect her agency in the future.

Both executive directors belong to the local HIV Contractor's Association, a lobbying group comprised of executive directors of all the agencies that contract with the county to provide HIV/AIDS services. In fact, Stop HIV and Contra SIDA have already collaborated on two projects during their membership in this contractor's association. At the June meeting of the association, they ran into each other in the parking lot and walked together to the meeting room. Unfortunately they arrived to find that the meeting had been canceled; a thick fog blanketing the area had tied up traffic for miles and the meeting had been rescheduled to a later date.

Always looking for an opportunity to connect with others who might help their organizations, Mary and Carmen decided not to return to their offices right away, but instead to use this time to have a cup of coffee at the corner café and catch up with each other. Mary commented on the recent announcement by a large local AIDS services provider organization of its plans to merge with an organization that did not provide such services. A conversation ensued about mergers, and by the time they were ready to go back to their offices, the two executive directors were talking about whether it might make sense for them to consider some type of partnership that went beyond just a collaborative arrangement. Carmen mentioned that she had recently attended a presentation on strategic restructuring, and shared with Mary some of what she had learned. Together they wrote down several reasons why it would make sense to work more closely together.

Two days later, after Mary had conducted some research on strategic restructuring, she called Carmen. After discussing and sharing ideas about strategic restructuring, they decided to bring the topic to their respective boards for discussion at their July meetings. Their hope was that their boards would become interested in exploring the possibility for a closer partnership, since the two agencies provided such similar services and faced such similar challenges.

Community Arts Center and Museum of Art and Culture

Community Arts Center is a $1.1 million museum and arts center serving the Springtown metro area. Its mission is to encourage and showcase the work of local artists, as well as to educate the community about the inherent value of diverse forms of art. Community Arts Center currently has one permanent exhibit, but otherwise rotates shows featuring the work of multiple artists (who all work in different media with vastly different styles). Community Arts Center also provides art classes to students of all ages and offers studio space for up to four fledgling artists at a time. The board, while more diverse than it was several years ago, is still largely filled with local artists and faculty from the art departments of two local universities. They are an enthusiastic group, but some members are starting to burn out with the constant struggle to raise the funds needed to keep Community Arts Center healthy. With less and less government and foundation funding available each year, that struggle is only getting harder.

In a nutshell...

Community Arts Center and Museum of Art and Culture

The agencies share a mission focus, but their strategies differ markedly. Each agency is currently being challenged by program development or financial issues the other agency has successfully navigated. The executive directors discuss the idea of merging, and even though they're aware of the potential resistance they may encounter, they agree to present the idea to their boards.

Museum of Art and Culture is an $8 million museum located in downtown Springtown. Museum of Art and Culture has several permanent exhibits, but is also a well-respected host of many traveling exhibits. While Museum of Art and Culture has an excellent reputation in the state, it is seen as somewhat aloof from both the local art scene and the local community. It has a strong board of directors that has raised a considerable amount of money for a new wing and a respectable endowment. Unfortunately Museum of Art and Culture's efforts to start community-based programs (including art appreciation classes, "Evening with an Artist" events, and school-based programs) have not met with great success. As Ron Kyle, the museum's new executive director, explained in a management meeting recently, "The average Joe and Jane just don't see us as being for them. Our reputation has shifted over the years, and while we still get a lot of visitors and donations from the upper- and upper-middle class population, the rest of the community sees us as being esoteric, and even a bit elitist. We're not reaching the full spectrum of the community with our services."

Community Arts Center's executive director, Marie Simeon, has been with the organization for almost seven years. While she guided Community Arts Center through considerable growth during the first five years of her tenure, she is concerned about the more recent *decline* in their budget (slight though it is), and is afraid that the board is "losing steam." Marie is unsure exactly what the best course of action might be, but she does have one idea. She has heard of several recent examples of arts organizations in her state that merged in order to strengthen their organizations and better serve the public. At Community Arts Center's last annual meeting (three months ago), one of her board members actually brought this up, and suggested that they learn more about the subject. Since then Marie has done some preliminary research, and has begun to think that a merger might indeed be a good option for Community Arts Center to explore.

After pondering this for a while, Marie decided to call Ron Kyle, the executive director of Museum of Art and Culture, and ask him to have lunch. Marie and Ron have known each other for years, though they have never had the opportunity to work closely together. At lunch the two executive directors talked about whether it might make sense to investigate the possibility of a merger. Both executive directors were wary of broaching the subject to their boards—there was some degree of rivalry between the two organizations, and Museum of Art and Culture's last executive director was very vocal about her lack of respect for Community Arts Center—but they realized that given the current climate, it might well be worth pursuing. After talking together for several hours, they agreed to go back to their individual boards and begin the process of exploration and self-assessment.

CHAPTER 1

Forms of Merger

What are the options for structuring your merger?

MERGER is a generic term for a kind of partnership in which two or more corporations decide to become one. The spirit and intent of these partnerships is to combine the control of the entities, centralizing it in one place. A merger is usually a wise choice when a high level of integration is necessary to the success of the merging organizations' strategic plans and when it is simply not possible to achieve this integration in lesser forms of partnership, such as joint programming, administrative consolidation, or a joint venture.

While the intent in a merger is fairly uniform, the means for implementing such a partnership vary. Under the banner of merger I include the following types of partnership:

- Outright mergers
- Asset transfers
- Interlocking boards
- Parent-subsidiary arrangements

Because these decisions have far-reaching consequences, it is essential that competent legal counsel, preferably a specialist in nonprofit corporate law, be consulted before a final choice is made and implemented

Each of these mechanisms offers different advantages and disadvantages. While the terms above may be foreign to many people, and may engender anxiety or carry certain connotations (both positive and negative), the choice of the proper structure for the partnership should be dictated by the needs of the organizations rather than emotional considerations. Because these decisions have far-reaching consequences, it is essential that competent legal counsel, preferably a specialist in nonprofit corporate law, be consulted before a final choice is made and implemented.

Following is a description of each of these forms of merger. Note that while having a basic understanding of these options is helpful when evaluating merger as a potential course of action, choosing between them is not necessary until much later in the process. Thus we offer general descriptions of the options in this chapter, but leave the discussion of how to choose the most appropriate option for your situation for Chapter 5.

Outright Merger

There are three variations for implementation of a full and outright merger. The most basic way to effect a merger is "merger by dissolution into." (This is known in some states as "consolidation.") Here you dissolve one of the corporations (the disappearing corporation), leaving its assets and liabilities to the other (the surviving corporation). One of the advantages of this approach is that it is clear to all participants and observers what has occurred. If, years later, a donor of the disappearing corporation dies, leaving money to that corporation in its old name and form, the estate can more easily find the successor corporation and pay out the bequest. A disadvantage of this method is that the surviving corporation assumes the disappearing corporation's debts and other liabilities, some of which, such as lawsuits, may not have been disclosed during the negotiations process. These "contingent liabilities" may in fact not even have been disclosable, because they were not yet filed (and thus not yet known) at the time of merger.

A second option is to simply dissolve one corporation, as if it were going out of business. Federal law dictates that no individual can benefit from the proceeds of a nonprofit 501(c)(3) organization, even in dissolution. Moreover, most state law provides that in the case of the dissolution of a nonprofit corporation, any remaining assets must be transferred to a nonprofit that is similar in mission. The assets could be transferred to a merger partner that fits this description.

The advantage of this option is that it may limit the surviving corporation's liability for the disappearing corporation's debts. It may also limit other liabilities such as potential lawsuits. The disappearing corporation may in fact be required to go through bankruptcy proceedings prior to dissolution, but if it is, at least its debts will be settled. Obviously, in a bankruptcy scenario, it is unlikely that any cash assets will remain to be passed on to the surviving corporation. However, other valuable assets—an organization's name, donor records, and possibly its government contracts—can often be passed on to another corporation. A disadvantage here is apparent in the situation cited earlier, where the donor leaves a bequest in the name of the now long-ago dissolved corporation. The administrator of the bequest may not find a clear legal trail leading it to the successor corporation. Thus the successor corporation could miss out on the bequest.

A third variation on this theme often appears at first to be the most reasonable, but is usually the least desirable method to achieve merger. This approach has both corporations dissolving by merger into a new third corporation. This option is sometimes chosen because of the reluctance of either partner to be the corporation that dissolves while the other survives. Unfortunately, this solution can cost the organizations dearly. It can take as long as a year to create the new entity and gain an IRS exemption; in the meantime both frustration and legal fees will mount. Thus, this variation offers few practical advantages, but does offer plenty of headaches, and should be avoided if at all possible.

Figure 2, Implementing a Merger, illustrates each of these three forms of outright merger.

Figure 2. Implementing a Merger

A. Merger by "dissolution into"

B. Merger by dissolution, with assets left to the surviving corporation after liabilities are disposed of

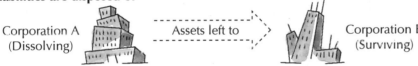

C. Merger by "dissolution into," with both parties dissolving into a new corporation

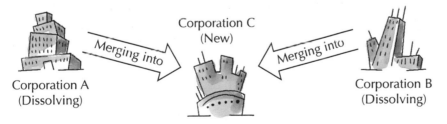

Asset Transfer

Asset transfers are transactions in which the corporations remain separate, but the valuable assets of one corporation, which may include money and real property as well as a name or other intangibles, are "purchased" by the other. This purchase may be for cash, but is commonly for some other consideration, such as a commitment to continue the organization's mission, to preserve its archives or art works, or to raise money for its programs. Asset transfer is illustrated in Figure 3.

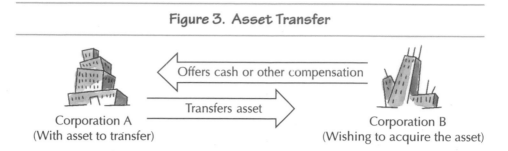

Figure 3. Asset Transfer

Offers cash or other compensation

Transfers asset

Corporation A
(With asset to transfer)

Corporation B
(Wishing to acquire the asset)

Obviously, not all of a corporation's assets need be purchased in an asset transfer. As an example, in one situation a college "purchased" the archives of another nonprofit in exchange for a commitment to preserve and curate the papers. No money changed hands.

Asset transfers allow the corporations involved to remain independent after the "merger." Sometimes this is for legal reasons only, and all that is left of one of the organizations is its corporate shell. In other cases, the organization transferring the assets keeps up some level of activity after the transaction, perhaps to pursue a specific program or function that the merger partner was not interested in acquiring.

Interlocking Boards

Two organizations may desire to merge, but for technical reasons need to keep the two corporations alive for at least some time into the future. The quickest and easiest way to "merge" these two nonprofits is to create interlocking boards. The parties can accomplish this goal by simply reconfiguring their boards so that the same group of individuals now makes up both boards. There are still two separate corporations, but the boards have the same membership. The boards, once constituted as interlocking, are then free to appoint a joint executive director for both organizations.

The advantages of interlocking boards are the ease with which they can be created (they require legal advice but no actual legal paperwork) and the speed with which this can occur. Occasionally nonprofits need or desire to merge immediately, and are not able to wait for the legal paperwork of a dissolution or merger to be completed. In such cases interlocking boards can be used as an intermediary step, assuring unified control of the organizations in the short term, until they become one on the corporate level, when the merger is legally accomplished. Figure 4 illustrates interlocking boards.

Figure 4. Interlocking Boards

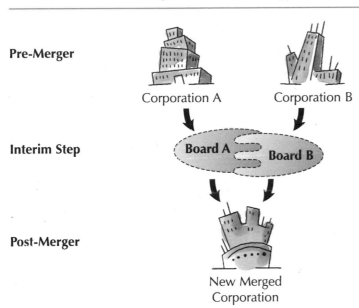

Pre-Merger

Corporation A   Corporation B

Interim Step

Board A   Board B

Post-Merger

New Merged
Corporation

There are several disadvantages to the use of interlocking boards. If you maintain two separate entities, you will need insurance for both, payroll for both, audits of both, tax returns for both. As noted earlier, these costs may well negate any potential savings from the merger, as well as complicating management tasks. Another more subtle disadvantage of this model occurs when it is used not as an interim step before merger, but as the final step in itself. This is sometimes done because it is so easy to create interlocking boards. In the short term everything may run smoothly, so there may be little motivation to pursue the legal processes required to fully merge. (Especially since these legal processes are often considered to be more difficult or onerous than they really are.) As a result, what was intended as an interim step becomes, de facto, the final step.

Interlocking boards create only loosely coupled entities

There *is* a problem, however. In such a situation there is the potential for one board to develop, over time, different membership than the other. For example, a new board member may be recruited who does not want to serve on both boards. Over time, this can lead to significant differences in the membership of the interlocking boards. If there should be a disagreement between the two boards after this has occurred, nothing prevents the corporations from parting ways. There is no legal mechanism for keeping them together. Thus, it is important to note that interlocking boards, while easily and quickly accomplished, create only loosely coupled entities. It is a great way to expedite the process and represents the best of the spirit of a merger, but should not be the first choice for a long-term arrangement.

Parent-Subsidiary Relationships

One way to prevent the possibility of the runaway board described in the previous section is to create the nonprofit equivalent of a parent-subsidiary relationship. This is accomplished most often by making one organization into a membership corporation and stipulating that it has only one member, the other organization. This is done by rewriting the bylaws.

One corporation rewrites its bylaws to state that it is a membership corporation (pursuant to the law in your state) and has only one member. It names the other corporation as that member. It should also state in the appropriate bylaws section (usually "Election of Directors") that the board of directors is elected by the membership (which of course is the other organization). Figure 5 illustrates this relationship.

Figure 5. Parent-Subsidiary Relationship

Before

Corporation A   Corporation B

After

Corporation A   Control   Corporation B
Parent/Member   *Subsidiary/Membership Organization*

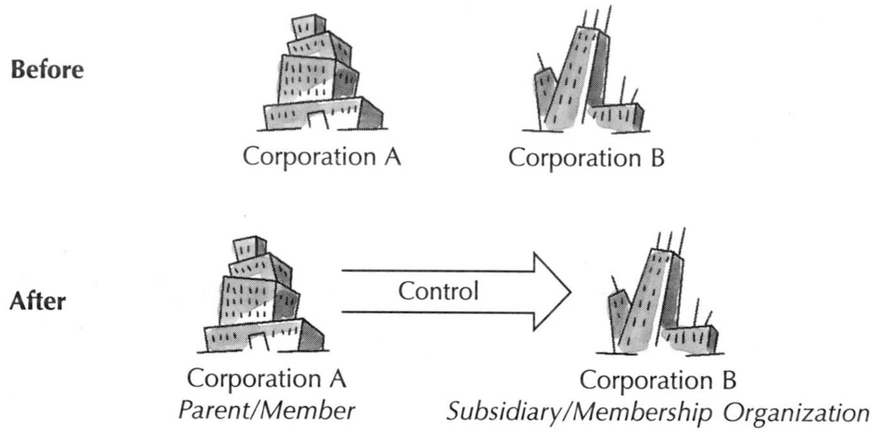

Such an arrangement gives control of the subsidiary, albeit at arm's length, to the parent corporation. If, for example, the subsidiary's board displeases the parent, the latter may remove the subsidiary's board and elect a new board, subject to whatever provisions are contained in the subsidiary's bylaws. The parent corporation, of course, also has indirect control over these and other bylaw provisions. One word of caution: Although the parent has legal control of the subsidiary, the latter may develop a political base of support independent of the former. If this occurs, it may be politically difficult for the parent to exercise its authority over its subsidiary.

Chapter Summary

Merger is a generic term for a kind of partnership in which two or more corporations decide to "become one." There are several ways to implement a merger:

- An *outright merger* can be accomplished by dissolving one corporation into another, by dissolving one corporation and leaving that corporation's assets to the other corporation, or by dissolving both corporations into a new corporation.

- An *asset transfer* is a transaction in which the corporations remain separate, but the valuable assets of one corporation are "purchased" by the other. Not all assets need be transferred.

- *Interlocking boards* is the quickest and easiest way to "merge" two nonprofits. This can be done either as an interim step or a final step, though the latter is not usually advisable.

- *Parent-subsidiary relationships* maintain both corporations, but give one "control" over the other.

CHAPTER 2

Internal Self-Assessment

What makes you a good candidate for a merger?

BEFORE plunging into any effort to form a partnership with another organization, the nonprofit leader is wise to undertake an assessment of his or her own organization's readiness and suitability as a partner. This assessment should be made in as objective a manner as possible, since experience tells us that the readiness factors described in this section correlate with success in the actual merger effort. It is far better to know your own weaknesses ahead of time than to have them pointed out to you by the other organization in the midst of negotiations.

Jumping into merger negotiations without first considering your own organization's strengths, weaknesses, and peculiarities is like walking along the edge of a cliff wearing a blindfold: it is dangerous, it can only complicate matters unnecessarily, and quite possibly it will make an already difficult situation much worse.

Jumping into merger negotiations without first considering your own organization's strengths, weaknesses, and peculiarities is like walking along the edge of a cliff wearing a blindfold

This chapter will help you answer eleven key questions about your organization. These questions are

1. What is motivating your desire to merge?
2. What do you expect from a merger?
3. Can you keep a focus on mission?
4. Do you have a unity of strategic purpose?
5. Can your leaders speak with one voice?
6. How solid are board-management relationships?
7. Are you currently in a crisis?
8. Do you have a history of successful risk taking?

9. Do you have a growth orientation?
10. Is there an opening in either executive position?
11. Do you know of other successful mergers?

Each of these questions is followed by a worksheet to help you clarify and document your answers. By the end of this chapter, you will have a clearer idea of whether merger makes sense for your organization.

1. What Is Motivating Your Desire to Merge?

It is important to recognize and make explicit your reasons for interest in a possible merger, both in general and with a specific partner if you have selected one. The earlier in the process this occurs the better. Sometimes merger processes can take on a life of their own, so it is important to put in writing for later reference why you are initially starting on this path. The motivations may be mission-related, economic, political, historical, or social, and are probably at least a little bit of each.

Strategic Motivations Mix
- *To improve finances*
- *To gain access to a larger skill set*
- *To enhance the organization's pursuit of mission*

Briefly, let's look at the common motivations for strategic restructuring in general and mergers in particular, and then try to determine where you fall.

Motivations for merger often come down to one or more of three overarching factors: finances, skill set, and mission.[6] The totality of these motivations might be called the "Strategic Motivations Mix." The elements of this mix have been distilled from the experiences of organizations in almost every sphere of nonprofit activity, representing dozens of actual mergers.

To improve finances

A nonprofit may desire to merge in order to forestall imminent financial collapse, to improve an uneven cash flow, to gain access to another group's investment capital, to fend off a real or projected competitive threat in the marketplace, or in an attempt to grow to a point that it achieves a leadership role in the marketplace and thus becomes the competitive threat itself. A smaller nonprofit with a solid program and a good but modest record of achievement may seek a merger with a larger organization that is cash-rich but program-poor in the area of the smaller nonprofit's specific expertise.

To gain access to a larger skill set

Through a particular partnership a nonprofit may seek specific opportunities for pooling resources and strengths in a range of possible areas: garnering media attention, expanding geographic limits, obtaining outstanding or specialized staff

---

[6] For a more in-depth discussion of the motivations for merger, consult some of the related works on the Resource List. (We have annotated the entries to assist in your search for the right resource.)

who are with another organization, expanding programming so that it is more comprehensive, creating a stronger board of directors, gaining access to donors and decision makers, and so forth. A nonprofit known for outstanding programming may seek a merger with another known for outstanding fundraising. The former group brings programmatic know-how to the table, while the latter can use the enhanced programming in its case statement to raise more money from donors.

To enhance the organization's pursuit of mission

A nonprofit may wish to reduce service confusion and fragmentation by providing its community with a single entity capable of much more than either of the predecessor organizations alone. This is often expressed as "avoiding confusion in the community," "creating a one-stop shop," or "bringing people together." Two nonprofits serving an underrepresented population may experience name and mission confusion in the eyes of donors, public funders, and even their own client community. Merging makes the confusion of identities work for the organization.

Often nonprofits face internal hurdles to self-assessment. It may be that the organization is badly divided, that the leadership is ignoring unpleasant financial news, or is simply overwhelmed by the press of other business. Whatever the reason, if the organization is unable to undertake a self-assessment, this is a strong indicator that it will have difficulty coping with the issues raised by discussion of a merger.

Worksheet 1, Motivators, on page 181, will help you determine your precise mix of motivations. A sample worksheet is on page 26.

2. What Do You Expect from a Merger?

Before you get into the thick of negotiations it is important to take a moment to specify what you hope to achieve from the effort. This exercise is best undertaken by a group of board leaders and senior managers. The more specific the outcomes the easier it will be later on, during merger negotiations, to assess whether the structure you intend to create can reasonably be expected to produce those outcomes. It will also be easier to measure the outcomes after the merger, years down the line.

Outcomes are best stated in measurable terms. For example:

- "We hope to achieve a 30 percent increase in overall revenues."
- "We expect to serve an additional five hundred people each year."
- "The merger will make us the largest provider of homeless services in the county."

Worksheet 2, Desired Outcomes, pages 183–184, will help you identify what you want out of a merger. A sample worksheet is on page 27.

Identify Motives for Merging

If you are currently engaged in the early stages of merger negotiations, try this exercise. Each organization's delegation to the merger negotiations should complete the next worksheet separately. When they are complete, exchange them with the other group. Are the desired outcomes very similar or complementary in nature? Or are they contradictory or mutually exclusive? The conversation that will ensue from this exercise could help clarify differences and thus advance the discussion.

WORKSHEET 1   Motivators

In practice, the motivation to consider a merger may stem from several factors, and these factors may overlap to some degree. What motivates your organization to consider a merger? Note that motivators are more general in nature than the specific outcomes you desire from the merger. (These are covered in the next worksheet.)

1. **We need to do something about our poor name recognition in the community. No one knows who we are or what we do. We're just too small to be seen.**

2. **We need to offer our clients a wider range of services in order to keep them with us. They're tired of chasing around town from one service to another. If we don't create a one-stop shop, someone else will and that's where our clients will go.**

3. **We need a new building and we're too small to raise the money on our own. We're also too small for any bank to loan us the money we would need to debt-finance the project.**

4. _____

Which of the three elements of the *Strategic Motivations Mix* (improving finances, gaining access to a larger skill set, or enhancing your pursuit of mission) best describes your own motivations, as expressed above? Is more than one type of motivator operating?

It seems that our motivators fall into the categories of needing better finances, and (to some extent) serving the community better through offering a wider array of services.

WORKSHEET 2   Desired Outcomes

Our highest priority outcomes for the merger are:

1.   **To develop a full continuum of services for our clients within two years, including child care, job training, employment counseling and placement, and a clothes closet, in addition to our current mental health counseling and substance abuse treatment programs.**

How will we measure accomplishment of this outcome?

   Through client satisfaction surveys we will ensure that by the end of 2001 we are offering satisfactory (at least!) service in each of the above areas.

2.   **To develop greater name recognition for our organization throughout the community.**

How will we measure accomplishment of this outcome?

   We will aim to get at least five mentions a year in local papers, on TV, or on the radio, and we will have at least one feature story appear during each holiday season.

3.   **To gain access to better fundraising, and increase the likelihood that we will be able to secure sufficient construction loans to meet our building needs.**

How will we measure accomplishment of this outcome?

   We will build a new building for our programs, in the heart of the community, within three years.

3. Can You Keep a Focus on Mission?

Many significant issues will arise in the course of negotiating and implementing a merger. Some will touch on areas where organizational leaders and other constituents have a great deal of emotional investment. In practice, the only way to move the organization forward through these myriad and often difficult issues is to keep everyone's eyes focused on the organization's social mission: the improvements in society that the organization was created to advance.

How flexible is the organization in pursuing its mission? Ask most nonprofit leaders for their organization's mission and they will instead tell you what the organization does.

- The director of a mental health center will say:
  "Our mission is to provide counseling services to low income children."

- The executive of a homeless shelter will tell you:
  "Our mission is to provide housing for as many people in need as we can."

- The managing director of a theater company will explain:
  "We exist to provide a venue for the greatest contemporary works of theater."

- The founder of a local environmental advocacy group will state:
  "Our mission is to stop the polluters from dumping toxic waste into our river."

Concentrate on Joint Mission

Whenever the merger negotiations committee reaches a particularly difficult point in its discussions, or comes upon a sticking point on a particular issue, ask everyone present to consider how the resolution of this point can advance the organizations' missions. The answer to this question should provide the guidance necessary to resolve the impasse.

These are not mission statements. Each is, rather, a statement of how the organization happens to pursue its mission today. If an organization stays in touch with the needs of its constituents, what it *does* may change over time. *Mission is a statement of the social ends these organizations and their programs strive to produce*: healthy children and families; hope among the hopeless; an enlightened and uplifted public; a sustainable future for the earth. These are possible elements of the missions of these organizations.

This is an important consideration because a merger often entails the creation of new programs, and perhaps most difficult, consolidation and change within existing programs. To the extent that your organization understands that its programs and services are not the same as its mission, and that the needs of the mission may in fact dictate changes in services, it will be better able to negotiate a partnership that retains what is most important to its success (advancement of the mission), and helps the rest of the organization to adapt.

Worksheet 3, Mission Statement, on page 185, helps you revisit your mission statement. A sample completed worksheet follows.

WORKSHEET 3   Mission Statement

As a group, recount your organization's mission statement. (It's okay to look it up if no one can remember it.)

The mission of the Sunny Times Children's Center is to provide intensive psychiatric day treatment services for seriously emotionally disturbed children by developing and sustaining an environment that promotes their growing maturity, family functioning, and the ability to someday return to regular school.

Hopefully, the essence of the statement can fit in the space provided. The shorter it is, the better. An overly long mission statement is sure to include information better articulated somewhere else. Moreover, the longer the mission statement, the less likely it is that anyone will be able to commit it to memory, which means that it will have limited usefulness.

Now rewrite the statement, deleting all references to services, programs, or how the mission is accomplished. Sometimes a clause will begin with the word "by" or "through," as in the statement "The Community Center is committed to ending poverty in our neighborhood, *through the provision of health and social services*." For this exercise you would delete the second half of the sentence, beginning with the word "through."

The mission of Sunny Times Children's Center is…seriously emotionally disturbed children…growing maturity, family functioning, and the ability to someday return to regular school.

You should now have boiled down your mission statement to its essence: a statement of what the organization is trying to accomplish. If it turns out that in following these instructions you deleted the entire mission statement (or close to it), then your mission statement is probably focused too much on service provision, and not enough on outcome. Try writing a new statement; one that contains no references to services or programs, and thus passes the above test.

The mission of Sunny Times Children's Center is to promote growing maturity, healthy family functioning, and a return to regular school for seriously emotionally disturbed children.

This restatement of your mission is what should be carried into discussions with your potential partner. If both organizations go through this exercise it will be easier to avoid getting stuck in a "mission rut" during negotiations. Instead of taking a stand in support of their beloved (and very specific) mission *statements* (a situation which can cause conflict over relatively minor wording differences), both organizations will be more open to discussing how the *essence* of their missions can best be advanced. It is this essence that is really each organization's reason for existence, after all, and it is more likely to be compatible with that of the other organization than a more specific, service-oriented statement.

The wordsmithing of the mission statement for the new (merged) organization can now be an attempt to incorporate the essence of the two original missions into one statement—a statement that still does not focus on programs.

4. Do You Have a Unity of Strategic Purpose?

Do the people in your organization share a sense of the critical issues that need to be addressed and, equally important, what must be done about them?

Does the board think the most significant issue facing the nonprofit is competition from a for-profit chain coming into town, while the executive director thinks it is the board's inability to raise money and position the nonprofit in the public lime-light, while many of the staff think it is the negative programmatic impact of too much change too fast? Are the strategies each group would suggest to address these conflicting priorities also in conflict?

Strategy serves to advance mission, and there is usually no stronger force in a well-functioning nonprofit than people's emotional attachment to the mission

In many organizations the conflict surrounding strategy and direction is not so neatly defined as in the examples just given. Rather than board vs. executive or executive vs. staff, there may be different camps within each group, and they may array themselves differently on different issues. Regardless of whether the conflict is between or within these groups (board, executive, and staff), if it is serious, it is probably based on value conflicts, different perceptions of what the constituency needs, or varying individual interests.

If the people in your nonprofit cannot agree on a reading of the environment and a coherent strategy to address opportunities and threats, chances are they will not be able to agree on the issues involved in merging with another nonprofit, let alone how to resolve them. Remember, strategy serves to advance mission, and there is usually no stronger force in a well-functioning nonprofit than people's emotional attachment to the mission. Merger is all about strategy: where to move next, how to move, and in what company. Thus, strategic differences will inevitably play out in merger negotiations.

These differences may already have risen to the level of obstructing the advance of the organization. If they haven't yet, they likely will in the future. Therefore, whether you move forward with merger talks or decide to postpone them, it is vitally important to your organization's future that these differences get aired, understood, and ultimately resolved and reconciled.

Worksheet 4, Critical Issues, on page 187, helps you ask your most important internal constituents what they perceive as most significant in the organization's future. (Note: If this were a strategic planning effort you would also insist that clients, patrons, donors, funders, and competitors be asked the same question. However, at this point you probably want to keep your merger discussions in-house. The point of this exercise is to identify internal differences that could impact the course of merger negotiations.)

A sample worksheet follows.

WORKSHEET 4   Critical Issues

List the top three critical issues facing your nonprofit, from the perspectives of the board, executive, management staff, and line staff. *Critical issues* are defined as those issues that are most significant to the organization's future success. These are the issues you *must* address. Don't make the mistake of guessing what each constituency thinks. Survey them, ask them in person, call a sample of people on the phone. Regardless of the outcome of the merger considerations, this exercise will be useful in that it will help you to identify the priorities and perspectives of crucial internal constituencies.

Board of directors

1. **How are we going to build a new facility for the dance program?**
2. **How can we raise $1 million for the endowment?**
3. **What will happen when the executive director retires in 3-5 years?**

Executive director

1. **Can we build a new dance facility?**
2. **How can we raise $1 million for the endowment?**
3. **What do we need to do to increase ticket sales by 10% each of the next 3 years?**

Management staff

1. **How can we keep the dance company together between shows, when there is no pay?**
2. **Can we mount a new Nutcracker, and what will it cost?**
3. **Is there some way to get a better benefits program for the staff?**

Line staff

1. **Are we going to go on tour this summer?**
2. **Will we ever get a better performance space?**
3. **How can we stay together between shows?**

Are there major differences in the critical issues identified by the different groups? Are the issues complementary or competing?

> **It seems that our issues are not so much in conflict as they are viewed from different perspectives. The dancers want a new theater as much as the board, and management and dancers both see a need to try to keep the company together year-round. We need to find a way to get everyone pulling together on these issues.**

5. Can Your Leaders Speak with One Voice?

In order for a nonprofit organization to negotiate with another entity it is essential that its leaders have the ability to speak and act in unison. This may seem obvious, but occasionally one subgroup of a nonprofit's board, management, or staff finds itself pursuing merger negotiations while another faction is either actively and publicly arguing against it or subtly and passively working to sabotage it. The result in either case is rarely pretty, and often quite embarrassing and damaging to the organization (and to its hapless partner).

To avoid this situation, organizational leaders must decide as a group whether to pursue the possibility of partnership. The discussions should be frank and open, clearing the air on all related issues. Of course, if underlying differences on organizational goals, strategy, and direction are present, this attempt to "speak with one voice" with respect to the partnership issue may bring them to the fore. If this occurs, these larger issues must be addressed *before* undertaking any action toward a merger.

Organizational leaders must decide as a group whether to pursue the possibility of partnership

Forthright disagreement and attempts to persuade others of one's viewpoint are entirely appropriate and even healthy during the discussion stage. Once a decision is made to move forward, however, organizational members who may be personally opposed to the decision, whether they be board or staff, are faced with the choice of either supporting the effort or resigning. The nonprofit board member's duty of loyalty precludes the right to express a "minority opinion" outside the boardroom. If the dissension is coming from executive or management staff, clear direction from the board, executive director, or both should suffice to present any dissidents with a similar choice between loyalty to the organization's position or resignation.

Some people may feel this ultimatum is a limitation of free speech. But the democratic process involves free and open discussion at all points leading up to a decision by majority vote. Minority rights are important to the nonprofit sector, but should not extend to a point where the minority is working publicly against the majority's position.

The foregoing makes clear the importance of a full and frank airing of the pluses and minuses of any proposed merger early in the process. Input from board, staff, and key volunteers should be sought early on. If the process moves forward, it may be appropriate to use town hall meetings, focus groups, surveys, and interviews to gauge the reaction of clients, constituents, and other interested parties. However, it bears repeating: Once the board makes the decision to move forward, staff and board members are not allowed to use any negative feelings about the merger that surface through efforts to gauge community opinion as a platform (or an excuse) to air their own negative views in public. (That this "rule" is often broken goes without saying, and also accounts for much conflict and discussion during merger negotiations.)

Worksheet 5, Internal Constituent Viewpoints, page 189, helps you survey internal constituents to determine whether the organization can speak with one voice. A sample worksheet follows.

WORKSHEET 5   Internal Constituent Viewpoints

Survey members of each of your four primary internal constituencies about their reaction to the merger opportunity you are currently considering. Once again, don't make the mistake of guessing what each constituency thinks. Survey them, ask them in person, call a sample of people on the phone. If you decide to go forward with a merger, it will be important to both understand these constituent viewpoints, and ensure that everyone in your organization "speaks with one voice" throughout the process.

After discussion, rate each constituency's reaction to the following statements. (You may either list all responses in the chart below, or average the responses to each statement for each constituency.)

1	2	3	4	5
Strongly Agree	Agree	Neutral	Disagree	Strongly Disagree

	Board of Directors	Executive Director	Management Staff	Line Staff
1. A merger with this partner is a good idea.	3	2	1	2
2. I feel good about this process.	2	3	2	(4)
3. I look forward to staying on after the merger.	3	3	1	2
4. I will support the board's decision whether I agree or not.	3	2	1	1
5. Mergers are the wave of the future in our field.	2	2	1	3

Any rating above a 3, if expressed by a significant number of individuals from any constituency, is cause for concern. Try to determine what is behind any negative feelings. Is it lack of information? Fear of the unknown? Dislike of the other group?

Can the negativity be addressed and remedied by fostering greater familiarity with the other group? Through joint meetings or joint task forces? Through better communication about the identified motivators, desired outcomes, or the process?

Discussion with line staff revealed a lot of uncertainty about the process, and some nervousness about what will happen to our programs should a merger be realized. We need to be more open and timely in our communication and make sure to make time for people to ask questions at the regular staff meetings, as well as the special monthly update meetings.

6. How Solid Are Board-Management Relationships?

One of the keys to a successfully functioning nonprofit organization is the presence of a smooth working relationship between the board of directors and staff, especially between the board and management, and most particularly between the board president and the executive director.

It is not good enough for both the board and staff to have competent leaders. This must be a "given." These leaders must also respect one another, offer mutual support, share a passion for the nonprofit's mission, and find ways both large and small to collaborate for the greater good of the organization. In the context of merger discussions, any differences, dislikes, or rough edges in this relationship can become exacerbated and, ultimately, undermine the entire process.

Worse still, long submerged differences and dislikes that are brought to the surface inadvertently through the merger process can tear the organization apart. This is one of the ways in which merger talks can lead to a questioning of the central beliefs and unspoken agreements of the organizations involved. Remember that submerged internal differences can come to the fore at any point in the process. Tread carefully here, and do not hesitate to get expert help in surfacing, sorting through, understanding, and working out any major conflicts, preferably *before* they erupt.

Worksheet 6, The Board-Management Relationship, page 191, helps you to uncover the existence of buried troubles. Since the questions on this worksheet are very sensitive, it might be best to distribute copies of it; the committee members should take the worksheet to their respective boards and ask all board members to participate. Answers can be given anonymously. The results can then be tabulated and reported in the aggregate only. (This is an excellent job for an independent consultant to take on.)

If the answers to the questions on this worksheet tend toward the negative, you have some work to do before trying to ally with another nonprofit. Conflict between board members and the executive director is always damaging to the advancement of the nonprofit's mission. Worse, if such conflict is routinely unstated and unacknowledged, it can fester and build for months or years, driving away good board members and staff alike.

In most cases, serious suppressed conflict will eventually come out in the open, sometimes with catastrophic consequences. Rather than trying to "wait out" the conflict ("the executive director will retire soon " or "his term as president is almost up") it is far better to recognize differences and animosities and to work forthrightly to resolve them. If that is not possible, it is usually still better to part company before a blowup that can tear the organization apart, leaving the executive director with a negative mark on his or her employment record, the board in factions, and the nonprofit in tatters.

Note: This worksheet can raise anxiety. It can also elicit less-than-candid responses: everything is reported as "fine" when it is not. Nevertheless, this exercise can help identify significant issues before negotiations begin.

WORKSHEET 6   The Board-Management Relationship

Answer the following questions as honestly as possible:

	Yes	No
1. Do members of our board of directors and our executive director get along?	☒	☐
2. Do they respect one another?	☒	☐
3. Do they routinely support one another?	☒	☐
4. Are disagreements and differences discussed openly and respectfully?	☒	☐

5. Think back to the last major decision the organization made; a decision big enough to involve both the board and the executive director. Did the way this decision was made exemplify board-management rapport, respect, and mutual support?   ☒   ☐

6. Who is really "in charge" at our nonprofit?

Probably the executive director, but she does communicate openly with the board.

Is the board satisfied with this arrangement?

Yes, because they are (and feel) consulted with regard to strategic decisions.

Is the executive director satisfied with this arrangement?

Yes. Her personality is such that she needs to "take the lead," but she doesn't hoard it.

Are other staff members satisfied with this arrangement?

Overall, yes, though a few people find the executive director a bit too aggressive and demanding.

7. Has the organization experienced high turnover in executive directors (more than once every four years)?

Prior to this executive director, there were 3 within a 5-year period. This exec has been with us for 4 years.

8. Do board members tend to leave before their term is over?

Not anymore—they did prior to about 3 years ago.

7. Are You Currently in a Crisis?

Organizations are composed of people, and people have limited energy and attention. If your organization is struggling with an acute cash shortage, coping with rapid growth, recovering from a recent public relations fiasco, or engaged in a major internal power struggle, it may not have the energy to focus on a new and challenging opportunity such as that represented by a potential merger. It might be better to wait until the crisis is resolved before embarking on anything so time and energy consuming.

On the other hand, many nonprofits are in chronic crisis: cash is always scarce, there has been a series of negative press stories over the years, or there is ongoing internal conflict that has been the norm for as long as anyone can remember. Ideally, such a nonprofit needs to set its house in order before it tries to ally with another organization. Otherwise, the organization's weakened position and lack of focused attention are only going to put it in the role of the weaker party in a merger that sees one player (the other party) calling all the shots.

A merger is a sort of crisis in itself, and as such can be useful in helping to unstick an organization and get it back on the road to solving its chronic problems

Nonetheless, the wait until such an organization emerges from its perpetual crisis could indeed be a long one. In the meantime, many plum opportunities related to possible mergers—new program growth, recruitment of a prized executive director, the addition of a well-connected board member—may be missed. Sometimes an organization must simply jump at a once-in-a-lifetime opportunity, even if it knows it is currently not able to put its best foot forward. But please, have no illusions of your position in this situation or of how difficult the execution of the partnership may be.

If you find yourself in this unhappy situation, try to use it to your advantage. Chronic problems have a way of becoming comfortable; everyone gets used to them as they seem unsolvable anyway. The opportunities presented by a potential merger may be enough to shake the organization out of its acceptance of the chronic problem and into action to resolve it, one way or another. For example, the ongoing sniping of the board and executive director, which can be an embarrassment in merger negotiations with another organization, may finally be addressed through a conscious effort to resolve the differences openly. Similarly, the cash flow difficulties that are hampering everything and threaten to derail a very interesting merger possibility may finally bring to a head the issue of getting expenses in line with revenues.

A merger is a sort of crisis in itself, and as such can be useful in helping to unstick an organization and get it back on the road to solving its chronic problems. Worksheet 7, Is Your Organization in Crisis Mode?, page 193, will help you analyze your current situation. A sample worksheet follows.

WORKSHEET 7   Is Your Organization in Crisis Mode?

Are you currently facing a crisis in your organization? There are many types of crises: an acute cash shortage, the unexpected departure of one or more key executives, the ramifications of huge or sudden growth, a public relations debacle, a major internal power struggle, and so forth. As a board, think about your organization's situation, and write down what crises (if any) you are facing right now.

1. **We are having severe budget difficulties—we are running a deficit, and will be facing a cash shortage beginning in 3 months. We have investigated all possible funding sources, but it looks like we may have to close down if we can't join forces with someone.**

2. **Our board is almost nonfunctional. At our last two meetings only one board member showed up. We only have four official members right now anyway...**

3. _____

Will you be able to resolve these crises before entering into merger discussions with another party? If not, how will they affect the process? Think both about how they will weaken your position, and how you might be able to compensate for this, or use it as an impetus to make changes in your organization.

> **We need to reconstitute the board before beginning discussions with any potential merger partners, as we need to have a board to spearhead either the merger or the closing of the agency. We can't fix the budget and cash flow problems before any discussions, but we can get some of the new board members to do a detailed analysis of our financial situation so we have something to show any potential partners. We will have to be honest about our situation with them, and understand that financially we are not very attractive as a partner. Instead, we need to stress our strong programs and our reputation in the community.**

8. Do You Have a History of Successful Risk-Taking?

Nonprofit managers often develop reputations within their community, their profession, and their industry. These reputations, while reflecting on the executive director's organization, usually derive from personality styles or quirks. For example:

- the conservative and prudent manager
- the wild west cowboy
- the clock-puncher
- the saint
- the entrepreneur
- the shameless opportunist

For better or for worse, these styles and reputations have an impact on the organization's behavior. Some organizations, following the lead of a conservative manager, become so risk-adverse as to be hidebound, while others, with a wild west cowboy (or cowgirl) in the saddle, are continually taking great risks.

Great risks often accompany potential rewards

If your organization has a reputation for succeeding at well-calculated risks, this is an indication that you will be able to handle the stress and risk of a merger. While it by no means guarantees success, and the lack of such a history does not preclude such undertakings, a tradition of successful risk-taking can be reassuring.

A merger is, if nothing else, a risk: the time devoted to negotiations and due diligence may in the end have been wasted; the organization you thought would make a great partner may turn out to be an albatross; the savings you have been counting on may not materialize; or the "temporary" tensions between the merging groups simply may not subside. Great risks often accompany great potential rewards, and sometimes the difference between those who reap the rewards and those who do not is the ability to stay on track while handling the risks, the downsides, and the setbacks.

Worksheet 8, Do You Have a Risk-Taking Orientation?, page 195, helps you review your organization's history with risks. A sample worksheet follows.

WORKSHEET 8   Do You Have a Risk-Taking Orientation?

Are you successful risk-takers? Recount three risky endeavors you undertook successfully.

1. **We built our organization as a coalition of major environmental groups who often have conflicts among themselves, but we have held together.**

2. **We took on the whole fishing industry and several reluctant governments and won the international oceans treaty, after years of struggle.**

3. _____

Are there other times when your organization undertook great risks, but did *not* succeed? What factors led to this lack of success?

We did try to work with another organization to create a joint climate monitoring system, but the effort failed. The biggest reason was lack of communication with the other organization—by two months into the project, neither party trusted the other, and our project teams were working at odds. We learned a good lesson from that one...

Was your organization more or less likely to take risks after these occasions?

Less likely, for a while, but people seem willing to move beyond that now.

Given its experiences with success and failure, how is your organization likely to respond to a merger?

We have a good shot at success if the partner and the opportunity are right.

9. Do You Have a Growth Orientation?

Successful nonprofits, like successful businesses, tend to be growth-oriented. Increasingly, nonprofits view growth as normal and healthy. Shunning growth may lead to staleness and may result in the organization's dollars stretching less far in future years. While an antigrowth ethos was once common among some nonprofits, recent problems such as marginalization, bankruptcy, and failure of smaller nonprofits has led some people to rethink size and to search for a scale appropriate to the mission of the nonprofit. For many nonprofits, this means growth.

Growth will probably be somewhere in the strategic motivations mix for the merger

An orientation toward growth is important because a merger almost always involves a growth-friendly strategy. Whether it is an effort to build a bigger and more diverse organization, to position the nonprofit to receive increased donations (which will in turn allow its programs to grow), or to build a new facility, growth will probably be somewhere in the strategic motivations mix for the merger. Another factor contributes to this as well: growth-friendly leaders tend to be open to new relationships and new ways of doing things. This flexibility is essential in merger situations.

In fact, some nonprofits have consciously decided that merger not only *entails growth*, but is in itself a strategy *for growth*. When it is difficult to obtain appropriate facilities, trained staff, and ongoing funding, merging with an organization that has these assets may be wise. It is often more reasonable, efficient, and feasible to "merge one's way" into a new field of service than to design and start up a program of one's own.

Tempering the growth aspirations of some nonprofit leaders is the need to consider ideal size and scope for a community, a type of service, or a field. A child care center serving one thousand preschoolers in one location is probably too big to offer the personalized care each child needs. On the other hand, a child care organization with twenty separate centers, each serving a maximum of fifty children, may be ideal, offering adequate size to allow for efficient administration and economies of scale, while preserving a small programmatic scale. Thus, overall organizational growth does not necessarily equate with individual program growth.

It is also important to recognize the difference between growth for the sake of growth and growth that is well thought out, appropriate, and strategic. The kind of growth described above can be extremely beneficial to an organization, and may indeed be necessary for long-term survival. However, those nonprofits that make it their practice to grow without thinking through the implications for things like service quality and financial stability can end up in a less-than-ideal situation.

While something may indeed be lost by the growth of a small organization into a large one (in particular the "family" feel and the sense of everyone knowing everyone else that can make working in a nonprofit so satisfying), these concerns must be balanced with the economic necessities that impel nonprofits toward growth. It is also important, here as elsewhere in the process, to examine the organization's mission and to position the nonprofit to best advance the cause for which it exists. There is no formula for determining the ideal size for a particular nonprofit; it is far too complex to reduce to an equation. However, you should be aware that any merger is probably going to entail growth, becoming part of a larger organization, and perhaps a period of years before you feel (if indeed you ever do), that things have gotten back to "normal."

Worksheet 9, Do You Have a Growth Orientation, page 197, helps you assess the organization's history with and attitude toward growth. A sample worksheet follows.

WORKSHEET 9   Do You Have a Growth Orientation?

What has been the percentage growth of your annual operating budget during each of the past five years, relative to the year immediately preceding? Express downsizing as a negative number (for example, express a 10% budget reduction as -10%).

		Year	Percentage Growth
This year over last year	(**1999** / **1998**)	**1999**	**12%**
Last year over the previous year	(**1998** / **1997**)	**1998**	**18%**
That year over the previous year	(**1997** / **1996**)	**1997**	**10%**
That year over the previous year	(**1996** / **1995**)	**1996**	**7%**
That year over the previous year	(**1995** / **1994**)	**1995**	**6%**
What do you anticipate to be the percentage growth of your annual operating budget for the next year?		**2000**	**13%**

                                                   Yes   No

1. Does your organization welcome growth? [x] [ ]

   Give an example: **We have added new programs each year for the past six years.**

2. Are your systems easily expandable to accommodate growth? [x] [ ]

   Give an example: **Our management information system is flexible and accommodates new data well.**

3. Does your board have a plan for incorporating new members? [x] [ ]

   Give an example: **Written in our policy guidelines.**

10. Is There an Opening in Either Executive Position?

One of the toughest problems a merger lays at the doorstep of negotiators is the choice of an executive to lead the combined organization. This problem will be easier to resolve if one or both organizations have a vacancy in the executive position, if one of the incumbents has plans to retire or leave in the near future, or if one would be happy with the number two position.

While the selection of the executive director is ultimately a decision for the board of the merged entity, this decision has such far-reaching consequences that it is wise to take into account the needs and interests of the current executives, managers, staff, clients, and the community. It is said that selection of a new executive director is the single most important act a board will be asked to carry out. Attempting to do so during a merger negotiation process is even more significant, and potentially more difficult. While the actual consideration of this topic may wait until later in the process, it is wise to think through your position now. Sometimes, after all other issues have been addressed, merger negotiations falter when the organizations discover irreconcilable differences over the selection of the next chief executive.

The most significant factor in the selection of the executive is the ability of the boards to work together in a spirit of mutual trust toward a mutual goal

Do you or your potential partner have a vacancy in the executive position? If one executive director is successful and committed to staying, while the partner organization is currently without a leader, you will likely be able to join forces more easily. This is particularly true if the incumbent executive is respected by the other organization. In fact, more than a few mergers are at least partially driven by the desire of one group to gain the other's executive director as its own leader.

If the selection of an executive director will be a necessary part of your merger, you will need to undertake a specific process to determine who will lead the organization. There are several ways to go about this. The board of the newly combined organization may choose either of the current executive directors to lead the new enterprise, or it may select another person to face that challenge. It can name the successful candidate right away, or it can embark on a search process. If it chooses to conduct a search for a new executive director, it can choose to invite the current executives to apply for the position, or it can discourage them from doing so. It can pursue any of these options on its own, or it can retain a consultant or search firm to help it. The one thing boards should never do is dodge the problem by creating codirectors, a solution that rarely works for long.

Whatever the board decides (and I have seen each of these scenarios played out), the most significant factor in the selection of the executive is the ability of the boards to work together in a spirit of mutual trust toward a mutual goal.

Worksheet 10, Leadership of the Merged Organization, page 199, helps you prepare for the selection of an executive to lead the new organization. A sample worksheet follows.

WORKSHEET 10   Leadership of the Merged Organization

This worksheet is best completed by each organization separately, prior to the start of negotiations. Once the negotiation process is underway, both parties can share their answers to this worksheet with the other, and together they can discuss how their ideas regarding choosing a leader might be compatible and how any differences could be resolved.

Indicate all of the acceptable ways to resolve the question of who will lead the merged organization:

- [x] Our current executive director takes the helm of the merged organization.

- [ ] Our partner's current executive director takes the helm of the merged organization.

- [ ] We ask the two incumbents to recommend which one of them should serve as the executive.

- [ ] Another staff person within one of the organizations takes the helm of the merged organization.

- [x] The two boards hold a joint selection process and decide between the two current executive directors.

- [x] The two boards hold a joint selection process and decide between the two current executive directors *and* outside candidates.

- [ ] The merged board chooses an executive director through a post-merger selection process.

- [ ] _____

- [ ] _____

11. Do You Know of Other Successful Mergers?

One way to gauge your organization's readiness to proceed is to determine its reaction to success stories from similar organizations. Do you know of any success stories? Could these "adult survivors of merger" talk to your leadership about their experience? Does your group respond positively or negatively to these stories? Do the stories motivate greater openness to risk-taking, or are they dismissed as either atypical or propaganda?

Worksheet 11, Success Stories, on page 201, helps you collect and preserve success stories from organizations that have merged in some way. A sample worksheet is on page 44.

WORKSHEET 11 · Success Stories

Record or identify stories of successful nonprofit mergers in your community or within your field. Is everyone in your organization aware of these success stories? If not, share them. They may prove inspirational, or at least reassuring, to those who are not clear on what a merger means or how it could be implemented.

Last year a youth mentoring program and an after-school program for children interested in learning about business merged to form FutureYouth. From what we saw it went really well. There was an article in the paper a few weeks ago talking about how FutureYouth now serves 30% more teens, and how the merger attracted two large local companies who now donate computers and employee volunteer time (paid!) for mentoring. Apparently the staff were really excited as well, as they now have better resources. There is still a lot of non-business–related mentoring (what the first group did prior to the merger), and that part of the program is growing, especially now that the community knows more about the program as a whole.

We should, in fact, tell the board and staff about this example; not everyone knows about it, and it might help them understand what we're trying to accomplish. Also, perhaps we could bring in a few people from FutureYouth who went through the merger to talk at one of our staff meetings? Let's get John on that—he knows one of the board members there.

Chapter Summary

Having completed the previous sections, you should now have some sense of how good a candidate for merger you would make. Consideration of some of the issues presented in the self-assessment can be uncomfortable, or sometimes downright painful. Nonetheless, the process you have just completed will not only make you more aware of your strong and weak points, it will contribute to the development of the internal working relationships and common understandings necessary for your team to successfully complete a merger, or anything else for that matter.

An organization will make a better candidate for a merger partner and will be more likely to carry such an endeavor to success when it:

- Knows what it wants to accomplish
- Is clear on its mission
- Understands and agrees upon its strategic challenges
- Is able, after full discussion and honest debate, to speak with one voice
- Has a strong positive board/management relationship
- Is not in crisis
- Has a history of successful risk-taking
- Is growth-oriented

Use Decision Tree 2 to help you summarize your conclusions and decide if a merger is indeed a good step for your organization.

Decision Tree 2. Is a Merger Right for Us?

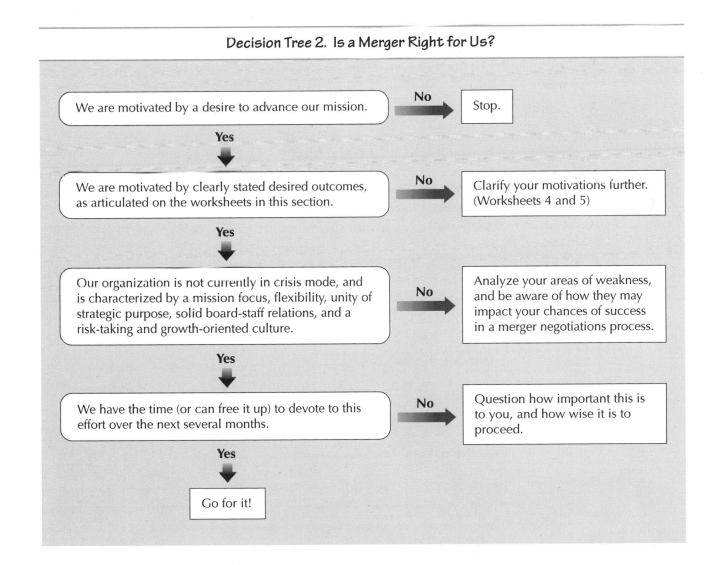

We are motivated by a desire to advance our mission. — **No** → Stop.

Yes

We are motivated by clearly stated desired outcomes, as articulated on the worksheets in this section. — **No** → Clarify your motivations further. (Worksheets 4 and 5)

Yes

Our organization is not currently in crisis mode, and is characterized by a mission focus, flexibility, unity of strategic purpose, solid board-staff relations, and a risk-taking and growth-oriented culture. — **No** → Analyze your areas of weakness, and be aware of how they may impact your chances of success in a merger negotiations process.

Yes

We have the time (or can free it up) to devote to this effort over the next several months. — **No** → Question how important this is to you, and how wise it is to proceed.

Yes

Go for it!

If your organization comes up short on one or more of these measures, do not read this as a sign that any attempt to merge with another organization will be futile. Far from it; weaknesses are usually only fatal when we are unaware of them. The management literature on this point stretches from ancient philosopher Lau Tzu to modern-day management guru Peter F. Drucker. By understanding your organization's strong and weak points, particularly in relation to a prospective merger, you will be in a better position to anticipate difficulties before they occur. This is really the most anyone can ever hope for in organizational life, after all!

Case Studies

Stop HIV and Contra SIDA

Enthusiastic about exploring the possibility of a more comprehensive partnership, both Mary (the executive director of Stop HIV) and Carmen (the executive director of Contra SIDA) agreed to initiate discussions on the subject at their respective July board meetings. The two executive directors also agreed to collect some information on mergers to give to their board members prior to the meeting, knowing that it would help everyone understand what the possibilities for a partnership might be.

When the days for the board meetings arrived, each executive director shared with her board the conversation she had had with her counterpart at the other organization, then asked for reactions. While the concept of joining forces appealed to both boards, they did not want to jump into an area which they knew little about. Mary and Carmen agreed to have their boards attend a joint presentation on nonprofit mergers. Mary contacted a management consultant and arranged for him to make a presentation on nonprofit mergers.

The presentation was well attended. It triggered a discussion on nonprofit mergers and whether Stop HIV and Contra SIDA should explore the benefits of a merger. Both boards agreed to discuss whether they would enter into formal negotiations.

Stop HIV and Contra SIDA were both motivated to merge by similar factors. First, they often competed for funding and donations with each other, as well as other HIV/AIDS service organizations. Second, they both recognized that eliminating unnecessary duplication could strengthen their current operations.

Each board identified several outcomes that they would like to see result from a merger. Stop HIV wanted to expand its services to include culturally competent HIV/AIDS services to Latinos. Though it stood on firm financial ground, Stop HIV also wanted to strengthen its current financial position. It hoped to consolidate its budget with another organization similar in size and in healthy financial condition, and then maintain a reserve at least three times as big as it did currently.

In a nutshell...

Stop HIV and Contra SIDA

Both boards of directors needed additional information on mergers. Following a presentation, they identified desired outcomes, critical issues, potential risks, and enthusiasm for growth. As Mary was nearing retirement, Carmen was seen as an excellent candidate to lead the merged organization. Each board committed itself to further discussions.

Contra SIDA wanted to improve its management information system, and hoped to use Stop HIV's sophisticated, computerized management information system. Contra SIDA also wanted to attract more board members with fundraising experience and contacts, perhaps by increasing its board size from nine to fifteen members within one year. The new members would have experience in fundraising, an almost uniform characteristic of the board membership at Stop HIV.

Contra SIDA's board was clear on its critical issues: attracting board members who were better fundraisers and improving the agency's management information system.

Stop HIV's internal constituencies felt that the agency's main critical issue was its upcoming executive transition, as Stop HIV's founding executive director was nearing retirement. Another critical issue for Stop HIV was the need for better-planned growth. Unplanned growth in the last three years had resulted in a visible decline in staff morale. Staff members had felt that the agency was growing only for growth's sake, without a plan, and that the staff and middle management had no input into the direction of such expansion.

This discontent at the staff level mirrored a growing conflict between the board and management at Stop HIV as well. Visible tension between two of the board members and the executive director dated back to when Stop HIV was much smaller and one of the board members was a client. Discussion revealed that most board members thought that Mary made the final decisions and that, while the board was not happy with this arrangement, it never did anything to change it.

On the Contra SIDA side, the relationship between board members and Carmen was cordial and friendly, but they disagreed about who really held the power. Lack of clarity and convoluted decision making were not uncommon at Contra SIDA. However, a common understanding of who is "in charge" would be essential as Contra SIDA moved forward, especially when high-stakes decisions needed to be made.

Both boards were comfortable with risk. Stop HIV had challenged the local government that threatened to cut off funding for HIV clients. Contra SIDA had consciously risked losing its special federal status by loaning some of its staff to rescue from shutdown a needle exchange program in the Latino barrio.

The Stop HIV board was enthusiastic about growth; it wanted to increase capacity and expand to serve the Latino community. The Contra SIDA board, however, expressed reservations that Contra SIDA's flavor and cultural focus would be weakened by merger with a mainstream group simply for growth's sake. Board members were worried that clients would be hurt in the process.

When discussing leadership, Stop HIV was concerned about Mary's upcoming retirement. But Mary was frank: "In light of the possibility of a merger, it might be a good time for me to consider retirement. After all, I *am* 63, and this is an issue that we'll all have to face sooner or later." Mary said she was fully behind any restructuring that would make Stop HIV better able to serve its clients. When asked about replacement ideas, Mary directed her board's attention to the current executive director of Contra SIDA: "I've known Carmen for years. She's a consummate professional with terrific interpersonal skills. I think she would make an outstanding candidate for my position."

When asked if anyone on the board knew of any merger success stories, Mark, the Stop HIV board treasurer, described the merger of his daughter's private school. It had merged with a similar school in an adjacent city to strengthen its financial position and expand its service area while creating economies of scale. "The first year of integration of the two campuses was tough going," he said. "But three years later the merged school is healthier and stronger, both financially and programmatically."

After much discussion, each board concluded independently that the agencies might be ready for merger, and committed itself to continued exploration.

Community Arts Center and Museum of Art and Culture

Marie Simeon (Community Arts Center) and Ron Kyle (Museum of Art and Culture) agreed to discuss merger with their respective boards, and they both did so at their next board meetings. Both boards agreed independently that while a merger with *some* organization might indeed be a good idea, it was premature to begin discussions with anyone specific. Instead, each board decided to go through a self-assessment process to determine what they might want to get out of such an effort, and what work they needed to do internally before pursuing it further.

Community Arts Center's board easily listed the motivators and desired outcomes for a merger. Jeanne Wu, Board President, summarized it this way: "We have a good reputation in the community. We offer high-quality programs and attract the best regional artists. We have *spirit*, and have always been praised as champions of creativity, diversity, and local artistry. But we're having a tough time raising money, and we just don't have access to either the capital or the donor base that we need." The board decided that stabilizing funding and expanding their class offerings were two primary goals, but that they must also retain their grassroots image and focus on freedom and diversity of artistic expression. They listed financial goals (including gaining an endowment of $5 million) and specific classes they wished to expand or include.

Community Arts Center's board was fairly happy with its mission discussion. While their mission statement did mention "showcasing the work of local artists," it was otherwise focused on *what* they were trying to accomplish, not how. The board members agreed to keep the "what" in the forefront of their minds as they moved forward (though there was unanimous agreement that focusing on local artists was of paramount importance to their mission).

The critical issues discussion was more surprising. While everyone surveyed agreed that Community Arts Center needed more exhibit space, line staff were more concerned with stabilizing class enrollment than was the board, which was unaware of the enrollment problem. Meanwhile, staff did not know of the financial difficulties so salient to the board and executive director. However, everyone wanted stability, ability to expand, and a wider reach into the community.

Next, Community Arts Center's board looked at how different constituents felt about the possibility of a merger. While everyone surveyed was at least moderately comfortable with the *idea* of a merger, well over half were very resistant to the possibility that the merger partner would be Museum of Art and Culture. Most likely, this reaction was due to past relations between the Community Arts Center and Museum of Art and Culture.

Everyone agreed that Marie and the board had a productive and satisfying relationship. At first the board insisted it would only agree to a merger if she would be the director. Marie herself reminded them that this might be too restrictive a condition. She said she might actually prefer to focus exclusively on education and community awareness. She *did* want to be involved, however, and made it clear that she would be committed to maintaining Community Arts Center's ties to the local arts community should a merger with Museum of Art and Culture occur. She cited the merger examples they had previously discussed, which showed that a smaller organization could retain its spirit even when merged with a larger one.

Community Arts Center saw itself as *constantly* taking risks—on new artists, new kinds of art, new classes (happily described as "running the gamut from bold to bizarre"), and new ways of reaching out to and supporting local artists. They also saw themselves as growth-oriented, though admitting that they had had difficulty in recent years reaching their goals for growth. Some board members restated the long-standing concern that too much growth could distance them from the pulse of the community.

Museum of Art and Culture's board went through a similar process with Ron and his senior staff, and found that their critical issues and motivators also pointed toward merger. Museum of Art and Culture had become more aloof from the community over the years, and was having trouble reaching out to local interests. Board members knew they needed to connect with the community, and they wanted to improve the museum's local image. They did *not* want to risk their reputation for high-quality, high-profile exhibits, however, and worried that merging with a "local" organization like Community Arts Center might do that. Museum of Art and Culture's desired outcomes were to provide a full range of art appreciation opportunities, including exhibits, classes, seminars, and off-site workshops; to improve its reputation in the local community and increase local support of its mission; and to open a new wing for smaller exhibits of local interest.

The board had discussed Museum of Art and Culture's mission on many occasions. It was "to present high-quality exhibits showcasing the outstanding art and cultural traditions of our country and our world," and there were already several board members who thought the mission was limiting. "We've tried other types of programming besides exhibits, and even if they haven't been overly successful, that's what we *want* to do," commented board member Marin Losee. "Shouldn't we take out the word 'exhibits'?" Simon Card, a local gallery owner, also pointed out that a merger with any organization focusing on local artists might necessitate changing the last phrase to include the local community.

While Museum of Art and Culture's board agreed that exploration of a merger was a good idea, several long-term board members stated they disdained "that contemporary art," and thought that association with Community Arts Center could only sully Museum of Art and Culture's reputation. "Local artists are great, if they're *artists,*" said Peter Banks. "But those Community Arts Center people call anyone an artist! We're about serious art, and I refuse to lose that. I just won't have it! Community art, indeed!" At this, several other board members exchanged knowing looks—this was Peter's style.

"Peter, that's a valid opinion, and we'll certainly discuss the pros and cons of working with Community Arts Center more," Marin said. "But please, we all need to remember that these discussions, as well as our individual opinions, need to stay within this group for the time being. And whatever the board decides, we all need to support that."

Peter grimaced. "Yes, yes, I know. But be aware that I *will* have more to say about this before any decision is made."

Ron was fairly new to the executive director position at Museum of Art and Culture; he had only arrived eight months earlier. So far, the board was pleased with Ron's work, and they trusted his judgment and willingness to work through strategic decisions with them. For his part, Ron occasionally got frustrated with the board's slow approach to change, and what he felt was at times a lack of creative vision. Still, they had made progress, and he was optimistic that they would continue to do so. He was honored when the board told him they would like him to continue as executive director regardless of what happened with a merger, and admitted to himself that he *was* interested in doing so. Still, the board president pointed out that they might have to be open to considering someone else if a merger were to occur, "though I'm sure that in the end we'd choose Ron anyway."

Museum of Art and Culture was not, the board admitted, an organization prone to risk-taking. It was interested in growth, however, and aggressive fundraising had helped it grow considerably over the years.

As a last point, Ron asked if anyone knew of any "success stories" involving mergers of arts organizations. Unfortunately no one did. Ron resolved to find such examples and share them with the board and staff as the process moved forward.

CHAPTER 3

Interorganizational Assessment

What makes a good partner for your organization?

NOW that you have assessed your own position as a potential merger participant, it is time to look at your existing relationship, if any, to a specific potential merger partner. The internal self-assessment probably highlighted some of your strengths as a merger partner, as well as a few weaknesses. It will save time and trouble later if you can determine now how those weaknesses might impact the course of the negotiations or implementation of an eventual merger. To do this you must take a closer look at your potential partner.

With some partners your organization's particular weaknesses could be irrelevant, or they could be the very reason you chose this partner. Some examples: you have cash flow problems and the partner is cash rich; your board is moribund but theirs is vibrant; you need a management information system and they have one.

With other partners your particular weaknesses might prove troublesome, but manageable. Some examples: your organization is divided on moving forward with the merger, but your partner is strong, steady, welcoming of the dialogue, and thus wins over the naysayers; you have an executive director who is a great marketer and fundraiser but leaves a trail of administrative disasters in his wake, while theirs is the consummate organizer who is perhaps too shy for effective fundraising.

In still other situations, your organization's weaknesses might be fatal in a merger situation. Some examples: your executive likes to periodically shake up the staff by reassigning employees to new roles, while their organization was built upon long years of stable, trusting working relationships; both your organization and your partner's are frequently unable to speak with one voice, and so tend to work against themselves; the volunteer board chair is the real power in your organization while the executive holds the power at your partner, and both of these individuals tend toward confrontation rather than negotiation to resolve differences.

Prior to the Identification of a Partner

Let's take a minute to consider the situation of the nonprofit that thinks a merger might be a good strategic move, but does not have a specific partner identified, or perhaps has several potential partners in mind.

This situation arises when strategic planning, market analysis, or other efforts lead a nonprofit to believe that it must integrate with another (perhaps a larger nonprofit, or a smaller, specialized niche provider) in order to compete effectively in the future. As the analysis of environmental factors becomes more routine in the nonprofit sector, this situation arises more frequently.

This is a golden opportunity to think through your motivations, goals, strengths, and weaknesses carefully, before you have a real partner to contend with

If your organization is interested in pursuing a merger but has no particular partner in mind, you should first go through the self-assessment process detailed in the previous chapter. This is actually a golden opportunity to think through your motivations, goals, strengths, and weaknesses carefully, before you have a real partner to contend with. Many nonprofits, finding themselves in the midst of merger talks and with a clock running for one reason or another, must rush through this process. You can take the time to do it well. Once you complete the self-assessment process, review the results and think about the type of partner that would best "fit" with your organization. Identify the skills, assets, and characteristics that this partner would have.

Next comes the task of seeking a potential partner. A client once hired me to locate potential merger partners through a confidential process. We were to identify and research organizations that might fit its criteria, which were quite broad. Because this activity could be perceived as predatory by other nonprofits, we were told not to reveal the identity of our client to anyone with whom we spoke. The need for confidentiality created distrust with every contact we identified, and we got nowhere. This approach to finding a partner turned out to be unworkable and was soon abandoned. (It was a good learning experience for me: I will never undertake such an assignment again!)

I now suggest to nonprofits in this situation that they use their usual communication channels to make a public statement of their openness to partnering, and let the highly reliable informal communication network (the technical term is "gossip") spread the word for them. The only downside to this approach is the tendency for the information you put out to get distorted. It is not uncommon for a nonprofit that thinks it is looking for a partner from a position of strength to hear itself portrayed as being in desperate straits.

Alternately, a nonprofit could take out the equivalent of a personals ad in either the local press or a trade publication. Such an ad usually takes the following form:

- Brief description of your organization
- A few bullets indicating what you are looking for
- Contact information

See Appendix C, page 163, for an example of such an announcement.

While an unusual step, this route has a lot to recommend it. It is very honest and direct, and it will reach many potential partners. The disadvantage, unfortunately, is that it is still a relatively rare practice and so may be met with distrust. Nonetheless, in the right publication, it could generate the kind of interest you seek. The approach has merit and we hope more nonprofits try it.

With an Identified Potential Partner

More commonly, a nonprofit organization's leadership has identified two or more potential partners and wonders how to determine which one to pursue with formal negotiations.

The keys to successfully handling an initial assessment period with multiple potential partners are forthrightness, speed, and courtesy. Keep each party informed about what you are doing and why; move with dispatch so that there is a minimum of time investment for any partner not selected; and remember your manners! Exhibit 1, How to Handle Multiple Potential Partners, on page 54, recounts a few points to keep in mind.

How do you first broach the topic of a potential merger with the appropriate representative of another nonprofit your organization is interested in, but who may not be aware of the interest? Often, the topic comes up as a point of mutual interest in a discussion between executive directors or board members from different organizations. If it does not, some brainstorming by your management team or board may turn up a person in your organization who has a contact at the other organization. Or, you might identify a third party with contacts at both organizations. Either contact might be an appropriate point for beginning a dialogue. If not, a cold call may be your last resort.

Understand, in either case, that the request to discuss a possible partnership may seem to be coming from out of left field. No matter how carefully you couch the suggestion, it may be perceived as threatening. Exhibit 2, The First Conversation with a Prospective Partner, on pages 54–55, suggests some important points to keep in mind as you prepare to broach the topic of merging with a leader from another organization.

Exhibit 1. How to Handle Multiple Potential Partners

1. It is best for everyone if you inform each organization that you are also having initial discussions with other groups. You should probably keep the names of the other groups confidential, but you could indicate how many there are.

2. Establish a timeline for the initial discussions. You want to choose a partner for serious negotiations as soon as possible. Dragging out the initial stage could lead to hard feelings on the part of those nonprofits that you do not choose.

3. Establish thresholds with each potential partner. What are the minimum requirements for a partner? Do they meet these? Remember, you are not undertaking full-blown merger talks at this point. Rather, you are trying to establish whether there is likely to be a good fit.

4. Once you determine which of your prospective partners is most likely to be a good match, inform the other interested parties immediately. Resist the temptation to leave them hanging while you negotiate with your preferred party. This could lead to resentment. It is better to tell these nonprofits (if it is in fact the case) that if the negotiations with the selected group do not work out you would like to return to them and ask if they are still interested in pursuing talks at that time. This will both preserve your credibility and show respect for their time and interest.

5. Never enter into full merger negotiations with more than one party at a time unless it is to be a multiparty merger. Consider the analogy to dating. It is fine to date around and see whom you like best, but, if you value your life, you should probably not get engaged to more than one person at the same time.

Exhibit 2. The First Conversation with a Prospective Partner

The first phone call

1. Make it clear that the suggestion that your organization and theirs might want to develop a closer relationship is tentative and that lots of thought would have to be given to the matter before moving forward. This will help your colleague at the other end of the conversation to feel that your organization is only a half-step further along in considering a merger than is his or her own organization, and that you do not have a hidden agenda.

2. Choose your words carefully. To initiate the conversation with "We would like to talk about a possible merger with your group," is perhaps too straightforward and may cause the other party to balk. You might better begin, "We think your organization and ours have a lot of common interests. We thought maybe some of us could get together and talk about ways we could work more closely." This leaves open the possibility that what you will come up with is something short of a merger, and will hopefully engage the other side in a conversation (which is, after all, your goal at this point).

3. Suggest an informal meeting of a few leaders from each side, perhaps at a board member's office, away from either organization. These leaders should be from the boards, with perhaps the executive directors involved. If staff initiate

the discussions, they should go back to the board to report as soon as possible. If they do not, the board may feel it has been left out of the loop and could therefore react negatively to the whole proposition.

4. Stress the need to keep the matter confidential until the boards have a chance to hear about it properly from the two people now on the phone. Rumor control begins as soon as you hang up.

5. Leave the conversation with an agreement to next steps. Perhaps you will both discuss the idea with a few trusted board contacts, or the executive committee and the executive director. Agree to talk again in a week or two.

6. Immediately after the call, write down your impressions and what you think the other organization's issues will be in considering a merger with you. Then report back to your board's leadership.

The first informal meeting

1. At the initial meeting try to focus most of your efforts on the interpersonal side of things. The content of the initial discussions is important, but it is more important that everyone leave this first meeting with a feeling that they would like to work with the other parties, or at least that they would look forward to seeing them again.

2. Discuss your organizations' histories, current challenges, strengths, and weaknesses. This discussion may not be as frank as it will need to become if negotiations move forward, but you will at least get a sense of the other organization's position on major issues such as fundraising, the board's role in governance, and the level of board-staff collaboration. You may also pick up on any conflicts among board members or between the board and the executive director.

Assessing a Potential Partner

Sizing up a potential partner is not easy and is never objective, but you can systematically ask yourself questions about the degree of trust between your organization and the potential partner, your past experiences, and the assets and skills they may bring to the match. The next sections and accompanying worksheets present some simple questions about your organization's relationship with and opinion of its potential merger partner.

Do you trust your potential partner?

Trust is a fragile commodity in the best of situations. It is ironic, indeed, that in the nonprofit sector, where so much of the work involves interpersonal connections, and where loyalties and trust (whether warranted or not) often are strong *within* an organization, there is such a low level of trust *between* organizations.

In most communities (either local geographic communities or regional or national communities of interest) the leaders and usually at least a few of the staff of nonprofits in the same field know each other. Often, however, the level of this knowledge is quite superficial: executive directors meet at conferences; staff speak over the phone when they have a client in common or need to coordinate reporting for a collaborative grant. Equally often, whatever opinions are formed about the people in the other organization, and thus about the organization itself, are based on secondhand information, gossip, and very limited real knowledge.

As the executive of a growing nonprofit organization in the 1980s I frequently recognized that, for good or ill, the view of my organization held by my peers at similar nonprofits was determined almost exclusively by their view of me. If they liked me, they assumed my organization did first-rate work. If they disliked or distrusted me, they assumed my organization had major problems. I noticed this tendency in myself: I thought more highly of the organizations whose executives I liked. This natural tendency leads to a lot of mistaken identities: organizations are classified in our minds without careful thought about their real qualities. I take the risk of belaboring this point because these generalizations may color your perceptions of potential partners more than you know.

If trust does not exist between you and your potential partners, is it because of negative experiences, ancient history that is gone but not forgotten, or simply a lack of interaction and thus opportunity to develop a trusting relationship? In all but the worst situations, the negotiations process can offer an opportunity to increase and build trust between organizational leaders as well as between their staffs. Most people working in a particular field have very similar values—saving the planet, educating children, stopping domestic violence, promoting the arts, for example. If these people get a chance to know one another better in an atmosphere that helps them to see their common interests, trust will grow. A willingness to work together toward the advancement of shared values and missions may well follow.

Worksheet 12, Do You Trust Your Potential Partner, pages 203–204, helps you honestly gauge your feelings about a group you're considering. A sample worksheet follows.

Do you know your partner and have a history of working successfully with them?

Nonprofits that consider mergers with one another often believe they know each other quite well. You may be longtime collaborators, competitors, or both; your staff may attend the same trainings; your executives may belong to the same association; and some of your board members may overlap or at least know each other socially.

But how well do you *really* know this other organization? Do you know its history, budget, programs, major funders, culture, and values? The better you know the organization now, the easier it will be to move forward. If your knowledge of the intended partner is sketchy, reserve a portion of an early meeting for each organization to provide an overview of itself to the other. Each organization should bring

WORKSHEET 12   Do You Trust Your Potential Partner?

What level of trust exists between your organization and your potential partner? We will refer to this number as your "trust score."

1	2	3	4	5
Distrust	Low trust	Moderate trust	High trust	Inadequate opportunity to build trust

List five experiences that have influenced the feelings of trust or distrust that led to your selection of a trust score.

1. **Our two organizations were formerly one. About ten years ago the board decided to close down operations in our part of the county. Some of us wanted to keep going so we split into two groups and we opened up a new organization under our name. How do we know that if we merge back into one organization the same thing won't happen again? The executive director is new, but how can we trust that the people here won't be abandoned again?**

2. **They want to merge with us because we have good programs, but what do we get out of it? We get calls from their clients all the time saying that they are unhappy with the services they provide, and asking us for help.**

3. _____

4. _____

5. _____

If your selection of a trust score was based on fewer than five incidents it might indicate that your view of your potential partner is colored more by feeling than reality.

We clearly have some trust issues that we need to work out with our potential partner. These must be addressed before we move into meaningful merger negotiations.

along a packet of brochures, press clippings, biographical sketches of key staff, and so forth—the kind of information you would pull together for prospective board members. In one sense, this is exactly what these people are.

If you know and trust each other, chances are you have a history of working together, either in a collaborative service provision arrangement or on an advocacy level. (In the human services, for example, it is common for even fierce competitors to come together in order to advocate for increased funds from their local government funder.) Obviously, a positive history will serve you well as you plan a closer relationship. However, if past experiences have been unsatisfying, there may be negative feelings and some outright prejudices against the other organization. You must address these concerns in the early stages of discussion.

A negative perception of another organization can often be traced to a specific historical event

As is the case with trust, history may be as much perception as reality. A negative perception of another organization can often be traced to a specific historical event. You may even discover that no direct participant in that event currently works in your nonprofit. Nonetheless, tradition can block questions about the accuracy of the organization's memory, or even its relevance to the current situation. Here as elsewhere, move toward the future. Ask, "If in fact none of *our* current people actually experienced the negative encounter with the other nonprofit, is it not possible that all of *their* offending people have also moved on?"

Trust, history, and knowledge of the other organization all serve a secondary purpose within a nonprofit. In addition to establishing agreement on our experiences, memories, and past, they help to define who *we* are and who is *other*. Thus, we hang on tenaciously to false concepts of the other, and sadly, we often look for the fault, the negative, and the dislikable that will confirm our expectations. For a merger to succeed we need not eliminate these human tendencies (even if we could), but we must understand them and dare to make them explicit. In doing so we take away their power.

Worksheet 13, Past Experience with Your Potential Partner, pages 205–206, helps you uncover the historical reasons for your perceptions of your partner. A sample worksheet follows.

What is the other organization's potential contribution?

Trust and knowledge of another organization are not sufficient motivation to actually merge with that organization.

Look at the items you cited as your organization's most highly desired outcomes from a merger (Worksheet 2) and your self-defined critical strategic issues (Worksheet 4). Does this partner bring the skills, strengths, contacts, and other resources you need to achieve your desired outcomes and to address your critical issues?

WORKSHEET 13   Past Experience with Your Potential Partner

List five ways in which you have worked with this particular potential partner in the past. Rate your overall satisfaction with the each experience.

1. **We fought for further funding from our county government together and won.**

Totally Dissatisfied	Not Satisfied	Neutral	Satisfied	*(Very Satisfied)*

2. **We developed similar management information system report formats for submission to our common funder. But they didn't really do any of the work—we did it all and handed it to them.**

Totally Dissatisfied	*(Not Satisfied)*	Neutral	Satisfied	Very Satisfied

3. **We developed a cross referral system for our clients to go from one service to the other. No one ever seems to use it, but it seemed like a good idea at the time.**

Totally Dissatisfied	Not Satisfied	*(Neutral)*	Satisfied	Very Satisfied

4. **We wrote a joint grant proposal for a collaborative effort to offer a new kind of service to our clients.**

Totally Dissatisfied	Not Satisfied	Neutral	*(Satisfied)*	Very Satisfied

5. _____

Totally Dissatisfied	Not Satisfied	Neutral	Satisfied	Very Satisfied

If you have a somewhat negative opinion of your potential partner but have less than five experiences listed here, it could be that your opinion is based more on the subjective than the objective. If this is the case, try to learn more about this organization. Face-to-face discussions can help to build a positive relationship where in the past absence and distance may have bred negativity.

To answer this question you must perform a clear-eyed assessment of the *usable* skills and resources of the other organization. By usable, I mean those skills that are more than merely apparent to the casual observer, but that actually can be put to practical use in your organization.

For example, the potential partner organization may have a much larger budget than yours, but that does not necessarily mean that it can or will bail you out. The larger budget may simply be the vehicle for creating a larger operating deficit. Alternately, most of the budget may be tied up in highly restricted grant funds, or the board may be conservative and not wish to risk the organization's resources. Similarly, the dynamic executive director you hoped to gain in a merger may be dynamite in the community, golden with funders, and charismatic from the speaker's podium, but constantly at odds with his or her board and staff.

You must perform a clear-eyed assessment of the usable skills and resources of the other organization

Are those apparent attributes (in the examples above, financial strength and a high- profile executive director) actually usable within your organization? If not, they are useless to you.

The search for usable skills and resources requires a level of analysis few nonprofits ever engage in. We are often enamored of the apparent or superficial attractions of the larger budget or the high-profile executive (to continue with these examples), but we do not take the time to evaluate whether they can be used to our advantage if we merge.

Using Worksheet 14, Usable Skills and Assets, page 207, make a list of what you believe to be the greatest skills and assets of your potential partner. Then take out Worksheets 2 and 4 and closely study your lists of desired outcomes and critical issues. Which of your potential partner's skills and assets would help you achieve your desired outcomes or address your critical issues? As you fill out the worksheet, try to imagine the conditions that would need to be present for the skills and assets on your list to be truly usable by your organization. For example, the larger budget of your partner will only be of use to your organization if:

a) the organization is financially healthy, and

b) the needs you want it to fund will be a high enough priority for the organization to motivate its leaders to expend their resources in this way.

In the second example, the skills of the high-profile executive director will only be usable in your organization if:

a) he or she believes in your mission as strongly as in that of his or her current organization, and

b) he or she is not only a great "outside person," but is also a skilled and sensitive leader for the board and staff.

On the other hand, there may be ways in which your organization's intervention can activate marginal resources of your potential partner. For example, you may have a great development director, but your organization's low profile fails to attract board members who can do major fundraising. Meanwhile, your potential partner may be known for having a board filled with high rollers who have failed on the development front. The combination of this board and your development director may create the kind of fundraising operation both organizations have dreamed of.

The message here is that your potential partner's most useful skills and resources will not necessarily come to you in a pretty package. You may need to use your imagination to predict what those resources might achieve when combined with your own. Finally, you must look with a cold stare for any superficially attractive skills or resources your potential partner possesses that will be of no use to you, and cross those off your list of reasons to merge.

A sample of Worksheet 14 is on page 62.

Chapter Summary

Knowledge and trust are key variables in all interorganizational relationships. Though you would probably not set out to consider a merger with a nonprofit you have only just become acquainted with, many nonprofits really have little more than a passing acquaintance with their colleagues and competitors.

This chapter was intended to make you more aware of your knowledge of and feelings toward your potential partner, and to help you understand the basis (or lack thereof) of these thoughts and reactions. It also dealt with the concept of usable skills and resources: attributes your partner brings *that you can make use of.*

If your knowledge, trust, and general satisfaction with a potential partner are less than fully positive, this may be a signal that a merger between your two entities is ill-fated. However, it may just as well mean that given the relatively little attention you have paid to this relationship, there is not an adequate basis for a decision in either direction. If this is the case, then it is time to visit the organization, read its materials, exchange staff "field trips," and generally open your ears to the word on the street about this nonprofit.

Do not be afraid to reject a potential merger partner because you have received negative information about it or have had a negative experience with it. Just do not allow prejudice, competition, or ancient history to cause you to reject a well-suited match unnecessarily.

WORKSHEET 14 Usable Skills and Assets

Make a list of what you believe to be the greatest assets of your potential partner. Then take out Worksheets 2 and 4 and study your lists of desired outcomes and critical issues. Which of your potential partner's skills and assets would help you achieve your desired outcomes, address your critical issues, or both? Under what conditions would those skills and assets truly be usable for your organization?

Your potential partner's skills/assets:	What desired outcome (D.O.) or critical issue (C.I.) is addressed by this skill/asset?	How is this skill/asset usable to you?
GREAT reputation; long history of contribution to the community; name recognition	**D.O.: We want to develop greater name recognition for our organization in our community.**	**If we use their name (or a name that sounds similar to theirs) the merged organization can capitalize on their reputation.**
Well-respected child care services for all ages and at multiple sites throughout the county	**D.O.: we want to build a full continuum of services within 2 years, including child care (we don't have any child care now).**	**As one organization we will be able to offer "our" services AND "theirs"— including child care, which we need.**
A large building downtown that they own outright	**C.I.: we need additional space for both offices and programs.**	**It's not—they already fill the building, and are pressed for space themselves. BUT together we may be able to leverage the equity.**
A strong board with a lot of "heavy hitters"	**C.I.: we are having trouble recruiting board members, and our board is too small right now.**	**More members of their board than ours will probably stay on, but as long as the board members are excited about our programs, we would end up with a strong board.**

Case Studies

Stop HIV and Contra SIDA

The exploration committees of both Stop HIV and Contra SIDA moved on to the interorganizational assessment phase of their exploration, leading the group discussions when the boards next met in September.

The Contra SIDA board began by discussing how much (or little) they trusted Stop HIV. One of the themes that emerged was Contra SIDA's fear of being gobbled up by a larger, more mainstream organization. After some discussion of this topic, the Contra SIDA board came to consensus that in order to trust another organization in a situation like this, the two parties would probably want to be assured equal status as merger negotiators.

Stop HIV had its own misgivings. Mary and other senior managers feared that Contra SIDA would take over Stop HIV's operations and strive to become a larger Contra SIDA instead of an integrated Contra SIDA/Stop HIV organization. The most vocal proponents of this position were the program director and the development coordinator. They had seen Contra SIDA staff and board members put down Stop HIV in public—and in front of funders—for not providing ethnic-specific services. They also described an incident where a senior Contra SIDA staff member had accused Stop HIV of enticing educated Latinos to work for Stop HIV or serve on its board. "This," the Contra SIDA staff member had angrily claimed, "continues to drain the pool of individuals who could serve Contra SIDA." After a lengthy discussion, the Stop HIV board agreed to stipulate that Stop HIV's current services could benefit from the integration of Latino-specific programs and that this was one of the motivations for Stop HIV to consider Contra SIDA as a merger partner. However, the Stop HIV board reiterated that it was also committed to assisting HIV/AIDS clients of other ethnicities.

Members of both organizations enjoyed discussing occasions when they had worked together successfully in the past. While acknowledging the success of their current collaborative ventures, each organization highlighted two previous endeavors that had been particularly rewarding. In 1997, both agencies successfully organized a citywide coalition to lobby council members to vote for the creation of clean-needle exchange programs in key locations throughout the city. The council vote was close, but Stop HIV and Contra SIDA emerged triumphant and held a joint press conference to announce the success and advocate the benefits of harm-reduction approaches for IV drug users. In 1998, Stop HIV and Contra SIDA successfully coordinated an HIV/AIDS summit for the region and kicked off a public awareness campaign aimed at increasing publicly funded HIV/AIDS services. Both agencies' public funding rose that year, as they gained more public sector contracts.

In a nutshell...

Stop HIV and Contra SIDA
Merger discussions entered an interorganizational assessment phase. Fears and misgivings were exposed and resolution strategies were formulated. Both agencies highlighted the successful collaborative ventures they shared, and decided they could be successful merger partners. An examination of Carmen's skills made her a strong candidate for the new executive director.

At the end of these discussions both the Contra SIDA board and the Stop HIV board concluded independently that they could be appropriate merger partners for each other. Contra SIDA saw Stop HIV's successful board recruitment program as a strength that could aid Contra SIDA in addressing its own recruitment issues. Also, Contra SIDA respected Stop HIV's management information system and saw it as a model that it would like to integrate with its own should a merger occur. The Stop HIV board, following its soon-to-retire executive director's recommendation, considered Carmen (the executive director of Contra SIDA) an excellent candidate for the position. In fact, the Stop HIV board was able to review Carmen's resume immediately, as she had applied for a management position with Stop HIV in the past and it was still on file. Stop HIV's board members were pleasantly surprised to find out about Carmen's expertise in organizational growth and development. This made her even more appealing to Stop HIV, in light of the agency's current growth issues. Finally, hiring a respected Latina as executive director would go a long way toward establishing Stop HIV's credibility as a diverse organization.

Community Arts Center and Museum of Art and Culture

Both Museum of Art and Culture and Community Arts Center were hesitant about entering into merger negotiations with each other, but both boards did agree that the two organizations seemed to have complementary needs and desires. They decided to learn more about each other, however, and to look more closely at their existing relationship. Ron offered to go to Community Arts Center's next board meeting to explain Museum of Art and Culture's programs and answer questions, and Marie did the same at Museum of Art and Culture's board meeting. In each case the visitor departed after making a presentation, leaving the board members to discuss their thoughts and work through the interorganizational assessment process.

Jackie Rhodes, Museum of Art and Culture board president, opened the discussion by asking whether people trusted Community Arts Center, and why they felt that way. Peter Banks quickly jumped in. "Trust them? Who knows. All I know is that they don't seem to be very discriminating in what they consider art!" That prompted other responses, and the ensuing discussion revealed that in reality, there had never been much opportunity to build trust. Museum of Art and Culture and Community Arts Center had always worked separately, and though Museum of Art and Culture's previous executive director had made some disparaging comments in public about Community Arts Center, board members agreed that she had done that to just about everyone at one time or another. No one knew of any particular incidents that might have justified her specific comments about Community Arts Center.

One board member, usually very quiet at meetings, sheepishly volunteered that she had sent all of her children to Community Arts Center classes over the years, and was very impressed with the organization. "I always thought they did quality educational work, but I admit I never thought of them as relating to *us* in any way."

In a nutshell...

Community Arts Center and Museum of Art and Culture

While acknowledging complementary needs and desires, these agencies decided they needed more information about each other. Presentations and discussions followed and the general level of trust improved. They each agreed to continue their merger considerations.

Another commented that he had always respected Community Arts Center's role in the community, but since his primary interests were history and nineteenth-century art, he had never taken the time to visit their sites or learn about their programs. "But then again, they *do* have a good reputation in town, and there must be a reason. Besides, when we look back at what we said we'd like to get out of a merger—they have that. They have the local connection, the experience in running educational programs, and a love for art. We just need to make sure they really *are* doing high-quality shows, and that they won't go off doing something crazy that would hurt *our* reputation."

The Community Arts Center board had a slightly more negative discussion. Several members of Community Arts Center's staff had heard the former executive director of Museum of Art and Culture give a speech where she referred to the need to bring more national-level art to the region, and expressed her opinion that funders had gone too far in funding the local, "quirky" efforts of places like Community Arts Center. But that executive director was gone, and Marie had a good relationship with Ron Kyle, the new executive director at Museum of Art and Culture. Board member Haile Zost summarized the discussion this way: "We all trust Marie, and if she says this guy is good, we'll take her word on that. We know they do good work—not *our* work, certainly, but it *is* fostering appreciation of another kind of art, which is also important. It sounds like our doubts aren't built on much, and that perhaps we should move forward with discussions. If they start sounding too high and mighty, or it looks like we'll lose our ability to focus on local artists and unique approaches to teaching and learning, then we'll back off." Everyone agreed.

CHAPTER 4

Anticipating Difficulties and Roadblocks

What are common problems in merger negotiations?

NONPROFITS entering into merger negotiations will find a myriad of barriers: some will be incidental, but some might be intentionally placed in their way by interests opposed to the merger. Some of these impediments may be potential deal breakers, others may be substantial but solvable, while still others may be simply annoyances.

Financial and legal liabilities, once uncovered, can be explained and understood, their level of risk assessed, and a decision made to move on or halt the process. Beyond these relatively black and white difficulties, a host of other issues and concerns often arise. Here are examples, all of which are actual quotes from former clients:

> *"I don't trust them; they are not telling the truth."*
>
> *"If they take over, we might as well just close up shop. We're dead."*
>
> *"Look at the mess they have made of their own house, you want them on our board?"*
>
> *"Their staff are untrainable."*
>
> *"Of course if we had all the money they have, we would have a nice building too!"*
>
> *"Their programs are awful."*
>
> *"They're just after our money. What's in it for us?"*

Distrust, dislike, fear, envy. These are not pretty, but they are pretty common in the early stages of merger talks. We have found, through experience, that these human concerns essentially spring from three sources: autonomy, self-interest, and culture clash. These sources of misfortune are small in number, but they are nonetheless pervasive and powerful. Every stumbling block we have encountered in the course of dozens of mergers is traceable to one of these three factors. These barriers, and ways to surmount them, are explored in this section. Familiarize yourself with them in advance, the better to identify and address them as they arise.[7]

Autonomy

Merger threatens autonomy, which is the lifeblood of most nonprofit organizations. In a sector offering low compensation, long hours, and the stress and uncertainty of continual fundraising, independence is one of very few rewards available

Autonomy is the lifeblood of most nonprofit organizations

to nonprofit leaders. In addition, nonprofits are usually founded by and often continue to operate on the commitment, energy, and drive of a small group of devoted leaders. These people have invested a great deal of themselves in building the organization, so naturally they feel a powerful sense of ownership. Most impasses in merger negotiations can be traced to inadequate attention to this emotional, and potentially explosive, issue.

Autonomy concerns are variously expressed as questions about the motives of the potential partner, the impact the merger will have on the quality of service delivery, or the loss of name, logo, reputation, or other intangibles associated with the organization.

Worksheet 15, Fears and Concerns about Autonomy, pages 209–210, asks key leaders to reveal the fears and concerns they have about loss of autonomy for the organization, its programs, or its people, and then, with the help of their colleagues, to articulate the advantages that might come in exchange for a lesser degree of autonomy. A sample worksheet follows.

Self-Interest

Whether it is board members fearing loss of attachment to a beloved organization or cause, or staff fearing loss of status or even loss of employment, self-interest is a legitimate and major issue that can lead to many breakdowns in merger negotiations.

Self-interest in itself is neither inappropriate nor unethical. Each person brings into the workplace his or her legitimate psychological needs for affiliation, security, and self-esteem, as well as the practical need for continued gainful employment. It is also natural to be concerned about large scale organizational change, and one's potential place in the organization after the change.

---

[7] This section is adapted from *Beyond Collaboration, Revised* by David La Piana. The James Irvine Foundation and National Center for Nonprofit Boards, 1998.

WORKSHEET 15   Fears and Concerns about Autonomy

Ask members of the board, staff, and management team to describe the fears and concerns they have about loss of autonomy for the organization, its programs, or its people. Discuss each issue thoroughly, attempting to clarify misunderstandings, create compromises, and articulate the advantages to be gained in exchange for a lesser degree of autonomy. If you prefer, recreate the worksheet on a flip chart for group use.

Fear or Concern	Response or Compensating gain from merger
Our name will change.	We might get better name recognition over time, and the proposed new name would give the community a better idea of what we do.
The quality of our programs may decline.	This might not be true. With better access to resources, we should be able to make some of the changes we've been talking about, and provide a more "seamless system" to clients.
"They" will tell us what to do.	Their management has a good reputation; maybe they know what they're doing. And maybe they want our input as well. We will be involved with implementation; we just need to make sure everyone's voice is heard.
All we have ever worked for will be lost.	Maybe it won't be—maybe we will be able to build on those accomplishments. We do know that we will be able to keep both the residental and day treatment facilities open continuously this way—something we can't guarantee now.
They are too big—the community perspective will be lost.	We will be financially stronger…and we can make an effort to stay focused on the community. We should talk to some larger organizations that still have a reputation for being "close to the ground"—maybe we can learn something from them.

Self-interest issues may arise for a board member whose mentally retarded child benefits from the organization's services; a board president who likes the power and influence the office confers; or staff members who fear for their roles or their very jobs. The challenge in a merger is to identify and address the legitimate self-interest needs of participants so that they do not move underground and reemerge as sabotage. This can best be accomplished by open and frank discussion, a quick resolution by the boards on the question of any job losses, and, in the case of staff, by a promise to provide a reasonable (preferably generous) severance package if for any reason separation becomes necessary. This is the carrot. The stick is often the explicit or implicit understanding that the severance offer is only good so long as the staff member supports the board's efforts and does not resort to sabotage, which, it can be made clear, will result in dismissal.

Identify and address the legitimate self-interest needs of participants so that they do not move underground and reemerge as sabotage

The person most likely to engage in sabotage is, not surprisingly, the executive director. Executive directors have both motive (fear of job loss or demotion) and opportunity (the executive is the organization's information hub) to sabotage merger discussions. Sabotage can take the form of bad-mouthing the other organization or its executive; foot-dragging in response to requests for information and action, either by the merger negotiations committee or the other organization; or dissemination of misinformation. Ironically, it is just these unproductive (if understandable) behaviors which, when uncovered (as they usually are), will help seal the fate of the executive who is concerned about his or her future with the organization.

Other staff may also engage in sabotage. However, the potential for this destructive behavior is usually manageable by the combination of clear communication about what is actually happening in the merger negotiations and a strong staff leader to guide the organization through the process.

Worksheet 16, Fears and Concerns about Self-Interest, pages 211–212, asks key leaders to reveal their self-interest concerns and fears about the merger, and then, with the help of their colleagues, to specify what steps the organizations or the merger negotiators might take to address these concerns. A sample worksheet follows.

Culture Clash

Corporate culture is a pervasive force in any organization. It is a shared set of customs and beliefs, sometimes stated as "the way we do things." Nonprofit corporate culture is revealed in the little things such as where staff sit at the conference table for meetings or whether they wear business suits or jeans to work, as well as in larger matters such as the ethnic makeup of the board, staff's shared political beliefs, and staff's and board's respective views of one another's roles and competencies. A nonprofit may have a weak balance sheet, but it will most likely have a strong corporate culture. (After all, corporate culture is free!) Surviving hard work and economic insecurity, absent financial incentives, requires a strong set of shared beliefs and practices.

WORKSHEET 16   Fears and Concerns about Self-Interest

Ask members of the board, staff, and management teams to answer the following questions:

- In what ways are your personal interests threatened by this partnership?
- What would help you to feel less threatened and more secure in moving forward?

As a group, complete the left-hand column, including the initials of any individual who is affected by a particular concern. Then return to the right-hand column and try to discover what steps the organizations could take to provide reassurance or clarification of each person's concern.

Who	Fear or Concern	Reassurance or Clarification sought
QT	I will lose my position to someone else.	Promise I can keep my position.
HP	I will lose my job.	Promise I can keep my job.
LA	We will lose our way of life here.	Arrange for us to meet and talk with the people we will be working with.
MP	We will lose our sense of attachment to the community.	Get community input before moving forward.
BK	I heard we will have fewer benefits.	Clarify any changes that will be made to the benefits package.

Corporate culture causes people from different organizations to have subtle differences in their perceptions. In the normal course of business this is usually not an issue, since visitors to an organization *know* they are visitors. However, during merger negotiations participants tend to forget this fact, to bring their own corporate culture to the negotiating table, and to expect others to share their understanding of things. This subtle shift in expectations occurs at just that point when each organization's most basic arrangements are being scrutinized, its very culture implicitly called into question.

Understanding and respecting cultural differences is no less important in merger discussions than it is when traveling to a foreign land

Worksheet 17, Organizational Culture, pages 213–214, provides a window into the unspoken cultural assumptions and traditions any nonprofit will have developed. Understanding and respecting cultural differences is no less important in merger discussions than it is when traveling to a foreign land. Each organization should complete Worksheet 17, and then both should use the worksheet to discuss their cultures. Talk about any cultural elements you may have in common, what values you share, and what values and rituals you want to bring to the new organization. A sample of Worksheet 17 follows.

Chapter Summary

Nonprofits entering into merger negotiations will find a myriad of barriers. Many will be incidental, of a practical (financial or legal) nature, or easily explained and understood. Many others stem from more human (political and emotional) issues, however, and can be difficult to address. We have found that these human concerns essentially spring from three sources: autonomy, self-interest, and culture clash. Concerns around loss of autonomy and self-interest tend to appear in the early stages of exploration and in the negotiation process. Culture clash, while often evident in negotiations, becomes more apparent after the merger is approved and the parties move into implementation. It is important to allow everyone to articulate and discuss their concerns around these issues throughout the entire process, and to address them in an open and honest manner.

Case Studies

Stop HIV and Contra SIDA

At the October board meeting Antonio, the Contra SIDA board president, scheduled an hour for a discussion of the merger exploration. The discussion began with each board member articulating his or her concerns about the agency's autonomy. The overall theme was that members felt vulnerable and even threatened by the possibility of being overpowered by the Stop HIV board. They also expressed concern about the possibility of losing some or all of their Latino focus.

WORKSHEET 17   Organizational Culture

Describe your organization's values, its heroes, and its cherished customs. Tell one story that is important in your organization's history. Discuss your completed worksheets with your potential partner to get a feel for the subtleties of the other's culture. Remember, much of what makes up an organization's culture is unspoken, but it is very much present and alive.

Our organization's values include:

1. **Putting people first: employees, members, and clients**
2. **Doing the best we can for our members**
3. **Being good stewards of the resources entrusted to us, both financial and human**
4. **Having a board that is respected, works hard, and is not feared by the employees**
5. **We always finish projects we start**

Our heroes are:

1. **Joe, our founder**
2. **Ian, an amazingly dedicated board member**
3. **Laura, who worked for our organization for 40 years, and was everyone's mother**
4.
5.

Some of our most cherished customs are:

1. **Beginning and ending meetings on time, no matter what**
2. **The annual all-staff meeting and appreciation day**
3. **The executive director's annual report to the board at the annual meeting**
4. **The staff softball game**
5. **Our ritual for saying good-bye to a departing staff member**

Tell a story that is important to your organization.

One of the most popular rock bands in the world offered to do a benefit concert for our organization. We had very little time to get ready but we held a press conference with the band and got lots of coverage. Then at the concert they handed us a check, on stage, for $175,000! Most of the senior staff and board members who attended couldn't believe they were in a rock concert, with the music blaring and the crowd screaming, but we did it and we got tons of media exposure, as well as a big check.

In a nutshell...

Stop HIV and Contra SIDA
Board discussions continued with a focus on autonomy, self-interest, board membership, and organizational cultures. Statistics were gathered on the delivery of services; fears were largely dispelled by this new information. The agencies became convinced of their complementarity.

The Stop HIV board followed a similar process at their October board meeting, but *their* main concern was that Contra SIDA's Latino emphasis would overpower Stop HIV's broad-based approach to service delivery, especially if Carmen were hired to lead the merged organization. Mark, the Stop HIV board treasurer, recalled again his experiences with his daughter's school merger. School A had a reputation for having a strong foreign language department and a large Latino student population. School B was seen as more mainstream. The merger negotiations brought forth some surprising information, however. School B's foreign language classes, especially Spanish, were actually of higher caliber than school A's, and school A did not have any more Latino students than school B. For years, "common knowledge" was made up of assumptions about these organizations that had no foundation in reality.

This story prompted the Stop HIV board to gather some statistics on the number of Latinos they presently served, and to compare these with Contra SIDA's numbers. The results were astounding: Contra SIDA served 68 percent Latino clients. Stop HIV served 58 percent Latino clients. The presumed difference in focus was not corroborated by the data. Mary shared a copy of the findings with Carmen, who forwarded it to her board members. Contra SIDA's board's fears about losing their Latino focus were largely dispelled by this new information.

Both boards also discussed self-interest concerns. The Contra SIDA board was concerned about employee salaries and benefits in a merger. Carmen, who had recently interviewed the executive director and board president of a newly merged organization in the area, reported that it seemed to be common practice to increase the salary and benefits of employees at the lower-paying organization to meet the levels of the higher-paying organization. "In our case," she explained, "we would need to adjust Contra SIDA's salaries and benefits up to the level of Stop HIV, as in most cases our compensation is lower." The differences were not great, and consequently the increased cost to the merged organization would be small, though still significant.

The Stop HIV board's discussions focused on issues of board membership. Two board members were interested in knowing how they could assure that there was equal representation from both agencies on the new entity's board. Also, they mentioned the need to increase representation from communities of color and from clients.

Each board then went on to discuss organizational culture. Their values, heroes, and stories were not in conflict. In fact, it was easy to see how they would complement each other. Contra SIDA's values emphasized respect for their clients and putting the client first in any decision. Stop HIV valued clients, too. Contra SIDA heroes were Ryan White, Cesar Chavez, clients, and student interns. Stop HIV's heroes were Ryan White, Martin Luther King, their clients, and their founding executive director.

Community Arts Center and Museum of Art and Culture

"If we're going to do this," Community Arts Center Board President Jeanne Wu said to Marie Simeon on the phone one day, "we might as well do it thoroughly. I think the board is ready to vote to move forward with discussions with Museum of Art and Culture, but first we need to talk as a group about our concerns. Then we'll be better prepared to present our priorities."

"I agree," said Marie, "and I'll recommend to Ron that he go through the same process with his board."

Community Arts Center's concerns centered largely around autonomy and the likelihood of culture clash. Community Arts Center had a good reputation, but that reputation had been built on a spirit of freedom to experiment with art, to take risks, and to stay "close to the ground" with the local art scene. Board members were worried that in becoming part of a larger, more mainstream organization, they would lose those assets. Specific concerns were that local artists would get edged out of exhibits, that Museum of Art and Culture would try to remove some of Community Arts Center's more experimental classes, and that Museum of Art and Culture wouldn't want to spend money on providing studio space for local artists. "It's also just the way they *are*," insisted one board member. "Our staff dresses down; they wear their paint-spattered pants to work if they want. And our hours are more flexible. They seem much more formal than us. Their board has more rich society people on it than artists, and they want to be seen as refined, not experimental. I want to make sure they're willing to adjust." On the up side, partnering with Museum of Art and Culture would make Community Arts Center more financially secure, and Museum of Art and Culture seemed to *want* to get more involved in art education. Museum of Art and Culture also had plans to expand, and could perhaps include a wing in its better-located building for some of Community Arts Center's exhibits.

Museum of Art and Culture had similar concerns about culture, with several of the more senior board members worrying that Community Arts Center didn't have the "dignity" that Museum of Art and Culture had. "Peter is right in a way," said one woman. "Community Arts Center's art is more, shall we say, *broad-based* than ours. I wouldn't want to cheapen what we offer. We need a strong reputation to continue attracting big shows."

Still, many board members admitted that they had always focused their efforts on a rather narrow audience, and that it might be time to change that. And it was clear that they couldn't draw the audience for classes that Community Arts Center could—they had tried, and it hadn't worked. There was also some concern among board members about what would happen to their own positions. Many had served for years and felt a strong connection to the organization. "Will half of us have to leave?" Marin asked.

Jackie responded that nothing was determined as yet, and that these concerns were all things that could be discussed and worked through in the negotiation process.

In a nutshell...

Community Arts Center and Museum of Art and Culture

Concern for the blending of the organizations' cultures continued to dominate the discussions. At the same time, their initial reasons to merge were compelling and they felt the negotiation process would resolve the concerns that remained.

CHAPTER 5

Negotiation Stages and Strategies

Is this partnership worth pursuing?
If it is, how do you negotiate a merger?

ONCE you have identified a potential merger opportunity, how should you proceed? How will you know if this marriage was meant to be? The four-step merger negotiations process described in this chapter will help you make a well-considered decision in a relatively short period of time. While there are often reasons to vary the process, it is a helpful and proven starting point. In addition to covering the most significant issues expeditiously, it provides a series of signposts that you can use to mark your progress along the way.

Figure 6 illustrates the process of negotiating and deciding on a merger. There are four steps in the process:

Step 1: Commit to Negotiations and Assemble Negotiations Committee

Step 2: Plan and Conduct Negotiations

Step 3: Write and Give Proposed Agreement to the Board

Step 4: Approve or Reject the Agreement

After an initial exploration of the idea, the boards of both organizations formally commit to good-faith negotiations (Step 1). They next form a merger negotiations committee, which resolves issues and performs the due diligence tasks (Step 2). The committee then makes its recommendations back to the boards, which alone are empowered to accept or reject a proposed merger (Step 3). If both boards accept the proposal, the legal process is put into motion and a merger is accomplished (Step 4).

Figure 6. The Merger Negotiations Process

Step 1: Commit to Negotiations and Assemble Negotiations Committee
- Two or more parties identify potential merger opportunity
- Boards decide whether or not to enter into negotiations
- Boards establish an ad hoc negotiations committee

Step 2: Plan and Conduct Negotiations
- Formal negotiations begin
- Issues identified
- Due diligence process undertaken

Step 3: Write and Give Proposed Agreement to the Board
- Committee disbands and brings its recommendation to the boards

Step 4: Approve or Reject the Agreement
- Boards meet to vote on the agreement
- If both boards are in agreement, merger moves forward

Step 1: Commit to Negotiations

As we saw in the previous chapter, most considerations of merger begin with informal discussions, perhaps between two acquaintances or colleagues who happen to serve on the boards of complementary organizations, or between the
respective executive directors. Eventually, consideration of the effort may mature
to a decision point: "Let's float the idea to our organizations." Next, a few board
and staff leaders at each nonprofit are informed of the talks and brought into the
discussions. Ultimately, these two groups may come to believe they are ready to
undertake a more formal process leading to a decision whether or not to merge. At
this point it is important to gain the authorization of the full board of
directors of each organization. Since only the respective boards of directors can approve any subsequent agreements negotiators might arrive at,
it is essential that the boards authorize the process that will lead to these
agreements.

*Merger is the quintessential
board responsibility*

The leaders of the fledgling merger effort, usually board chairs and executive directors, should bring the idea to their respective full boards, preceded by a one-
page overview of the reasons for interest in the partnership. This summary should
go out ahead of the discussion, perhaps as an attachment to the regular pre-board
meeting packet.

The board may reach a decision either in favor of or against entering into negotiations after only one short discussion, or it may take several meetings to reach a
decision. Sometimes the entire discussion is put on the back burner, only to reemerge months or even years later. However long it takes the board to act, it is
vitally important that as part of the decision process it articulates why the

organization is interested in the potential merger and what it hopes to get out of the partnership. This statement should be in writing, and the negotiators should be authorized to share it with their counterparts from the potential merger partner at the first negotiations committee meeting. (The sections on *Motivators* and *Outcomes*, earlier in this workbook, could help here.)

It is important at this point to tell the board that

- It is not presently being asked to authorize a merger, only a negotiations process

- It will be kept informed of the progress of the negotiations at each step

- It will ultimately be asked to vote on a proposed merger, if the committee can strike a deal

- It cannot and will not be committed to a merger without its specific authorization

In many nonprofits the executive director makes decisions and carries out negotiations of all kinds on behalf of the organization. She or he commits the organization to contracts; assures performance relative to grants received; decides on employment, promotion, and dismissal of personnel; and relates to vendors, other nonprofits, and funders, both public and private.

Merger, however, is a different sort of commitment. Along with founding or dissolving the corporation, hiring the executive director, and recruiting new board members to replace and renew itself, merger is the quintessential board responsibility. Therefore, although the executive director should play a central role in the process, the board must take the lead. Ultimately, this is the board's decision.

After discussion, the board should consider and vote to approve a resolution which does three things:

- Commits itself to good-faith negotiations toward a possible merger

- Establishes an ad hoc committee to carry out the negotiations and report back

- Sets a time period for the negotiations

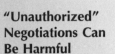

"Unauthorized" Negotiations Can Be Harmful

Don't let the initial "unauthorized" discussions among individuals (for example, the executive directors or a small group of board members) proceed too long or go too deep without taking the matter back to the entire board for its consideration. Nothing can turn a board sour on a recommendation so quickly as feeling that the negotiations have already begun and they are being asked to act as a rubber stamp.

Good-faith resolution

The good-faith resolution mentioned above might read:

ABC corporation commits itself for a period of six months to good-faith negotiations toward a potential merger with XYZ. During that time ABC will not enter into merger negotiations with a third party, nor will it make any material changes affecting the corporation, its leadership, or its financial commitments without fully informing, in advance, XYZ. ABC's delegation to the merger negotiations committee shall consist of our executive director and the following four board members: 1_____, 2_____, 3_____, 4_____. At the end of the above authorized negotiations period, if not sooner, the committee will submit its report and recommendations to the full board. The six-month time period may be extended by vote of the board, upon request by the negotiations committee.

While a simple majority of the board is all that is necessary to authorize this process, if such a resolution passes by a bare 51 percent margin (or, in practice, by anything short of overwhelming support), conflict may arise within the organization and there may be problems securing approval of an eventual merger agreement. Therefore, especially when support is less than unanimous, but even when it is quite unified, devote attention to educating the board on the reasons for the proposed affiliation as well as the terms being negotiated by the committee at each step along the way. If you wait until the agreement is done and then submit it for the board's approval all tied up with a bow, you may be in for a rude awakening.

The merger negotiations committee should probably include the executive directors and four to six board members from each organization.[8] In larger organizations, other senior management staff may be involved. It is important, however, that a bevy of well-informed full-time staff professionals *not* be allowed to either replace or displace the central role of the board in the process. One way to balance the staff's knowledge with the board's responsibility is to ask staff members other than the executive director to *support* the committee, providing reports, organizing logistics, answering questions, and ensuring communication, while the board members and the executive directors conduct the actual negotiations.

Milestone

Once the organizations' respective boards authorize negotiations, there should be sufficient unity of purpose within and among the organizations to move forward.

Often the delegation from each board is led by that board's chair. The composition of the negotiations committee should itself be negotiated with the other organization, so that there is equal representation, equal numbers of staff, and so forth. This may seem formalistic, and it is, but it helps to build trust right from the outset.

Confidentiality agreement

Merger negotiations require that potential partners share sensitive, confidential, or proprietary information with one another. For example, the due diligence process asks each party to disclose lawsuits, debts, and other obligations; staff integration negotiations usually involve sharing salary information for all employees; development staff may compare donor lists to determine the extent of overlap, sometimes a critical concern; your potential partner's finance people will likely want to

---

[8] In multiparty negotiations it may be wise to reduce this number, simply to keep the committee to a manageable size. The minimum number should never be less than two negotiators per organization—a board member and the executive director.

analyze your budget, balance sheet, and investments; and staff programmatic reviews may reveal unique service components or approaches.

You may not be guarding the secret formula for Coca Cola, but chances are you have a few critical strategic advantages you would rather not share with the world, and you certainly would not like to hear that *your* salary was being discussed by your colleagues and competitors in the community. Sharing this information is essential if the boards are to determine the appropriateness of a merger. But it is also scary, and potentially dangerous, if the merger does not, in the end, occur.

To address this well-founded fear, nonprofits discussing merger can enter into a confidentiality agreement: a statement of how information shared by the groups during negotiations and the due diligence process will be treated, both during negotiations and forever after. Many nonprofits agree verbally and very informally that "no information shared during the process will be leaked to any third party." While I have never seen a problem arise with these verbal agreements, it may be wise to put this understanding in writing and expand upon it.

Implementing some sort of agreement can help people of goodwill from both parties to act in good faith

Larger nonprofits will often ask their attorney to draft the confidentiality agreement for their consideration. These documents, which may look like business contracts, can run to several pages in length and be as obscure as any other legal document. Nonprofits not wishing to go to this length (and expense) might draw up a simple agreement. For a sample agreement, see Appendix D, Sample Confidentiality Agreement, page 165.

Whether you come to a verbal understanding, draw up your own agreement, or execute an agreement drafted by your attorney, it is important to note that no agreement of this type is airtight. Your best assurance is the integrity of the leaders of the other organization. Nonetheless, implementing some sort of agreement can help people of goodwill from both parties to act in good faith by making explicit their mutual understandings and responsibilities regarding confidential information.

Merger negotiations committee

A merger negotiations committee should be formed as the joint negotiating body created by the two organizations. This body should be viewed as one committee composed of people from two organizations, *not* two committees negotiating with each other. As observed earlier, merger negotiations committee members should be equal in number and type from the two groups. The committee need not, however, include solely the respective boards' executive committee members. A range of skills is needed by the committee; these skills should be sought anywhere the board might have them.

Board members with financial analysis skills, as well as those familiar with their particular nonprofit's financial condition, will be helpful with the due diligence phase of the negotiations; human resource specialists or experienced managers can assist in comparing practices between the two potential partners; board members with skills and contacts in insurance, real estate, labor law, and a host of other business specialties will also be useful to the process. It is essential to include board members who understand and are passionate about the mission of one or both of the organizations, those who can articulate a future vision, and those who are close to the community and can reflect its anxieties, if any, about the merger. Above all, committee members must be reasonable people who can negotiate in good faith. They will need tact, humor, patience, and an obvious commitment to the cause to help move the discussions over the inevitable rough spots.

As with any important board task, it is essential to choose members who will represent the organization well, who are trustworthy and intelligent, and who can be relied upon to follow through from meeting to meeting. Consistent attendance is crucial to moving the process forward, and should be a requirement of committee membership. If opinion on your board varies regarding the advisability of the merger, it may be wise to add a couple of reluctant or skeptical board members to the committee, so long as they are able to keep an open mind throughout the negotiations.

One caution both in forming the committee and in negotiating the merger: be aware that board members who have been through corporate mergers, or who are corporate attorneys, may have particularly strong feelings about the merger (pro or con) and about how it should be structured. Because nonprofit mergers derive from somewhat different motivations and are carried out for very different ends, these perspectives may be less than helpful. At the outset, it may be useful to explain to the merger negotiations committee some of the differences between corporate and nonprofit mergers. See the comparison in Exhibit 3, Comparison of Business and Nonprofit Mergers on the facing page.

Supportive "Externals" Can Play a Role

Occasionally one party will wish to bring in its own consultant, separate from any jointly hired consultant the parties may agree to hire as facilitator and guide for the process. This practice is borrowed from business, where consultants (usually attorneys or investment bankers) are hired by both sides to steer the process. While you should never try to prevent a potential partner from seeking advice, it is usually helpful if such an "agent" occupies the same role recommended for staff: She or he provides support for the organization throughout the process, but is not a negotiator or principal in the talks.

Reasonable time frame

Nonprofit mergers are notorious for taking an inordinate amount of time to negotiate, and longer still to implement. While this is frustrating, there are many good reasons for it. Mergers are complex undertakings that spawn new issues seemingly as quickly as old ones get resolved. The boards are composed of volunteers, staff already have full-time jobs, and the organization has a daily life that goes on unimpeded (hopefully) by the discussions.

Exhibit 3. Comparison of Business and Nonprofit Mergers[9]

	Business	**Nonprofit**
Motivation	• Raise share values	• Stronger financial position; forestall financial collapse
	• Increase profitability	• Better serve community; accomplish mission more effectively
	• Access a larger market	• Access a larger market
	• Improve competitiveness	• Improve competitiveness
	• Acquire talented staff	• Acquire talented staff
	• Access new technology	• Access new programs
	• Access capital	• Access capital, contracts, or funding sources
Authority	• Board	• Board
	• Chief Executive Officer	• Executive Director
	• Shareholders	• Members (in some nonprofits)
Money	• Fortunes to be made	• No personal gain
	• Golden parachutes	
Regulation	• Justice Department	• State Attorney General or Secretary of State
	• Securities Exchange Commission	• Internal Revenue Service
How it happens	• Acquire outstanding stock	• Voluntary agreement
	• Exchange stock	• Exchange board members
	• Acquire assets	• Acquire assets

Nonetheless, it is better to devote a substantial amount of time over a concentrated period than to allow the negotiations to drag on endlessly. Once the possibility of a merger is general knowledge in the organization and in the community (and this will happen sooner rather than later) anxieties will be aroused. Staff morale, and indeed the smooth functioning of the organization, requires a speedy resolution. Client uncertainty, funder worries, and board impatience all urge speedy action. In our experience, four to six months of active engagement by the parties is usually sufficient time to conclude negotiations.

Four to six months of active engagement is usually sufficient to conclude negotiations

Actual execution of a merger agreement can, of course, take much longer, and full implementation, including realization of all the hoped-for gains of the partnership, will take years. Interestingly, once an agreement is reached and an announcement made, board and community (but not staff) anxieties will subside. As long as the parties have reached an agreement, a longer time frame for implementation, while stressful for staff, is usually not damaging to the organization's public image.

[9] Adapted from *Nonprofit Mergers: The Board's Responsibility to Consider the Unthinkable* by David La Piana, National Center for Nonprofit Boards, 1994, p. 7.

Step 2: Plan and Conduct Negotiations

Once merger negotiations have been authorized and a negotiations committee has been formed, it is time to begin formal negotiations. The initial negotiations meeting should be scheduled for at least four to five hours. Subsequent meetings may vary in length, but the initial meeting requires sufficient time to set the agenda for the entire negotiations process. It also provides an opportunity for committee members to get acquainted.

Exhibit 4, Sample Agenda, below, shows a sample agenda for the first merger negotiation committee meeting.

If a consultant is used to facilitate the discussions, she or he should lead the meeting. If not, appoint one cochair from each organization. These cochairs should not

Exhibit 4. Sample Agenda for the First Merger Negotiations Committee Meeting

ABC and XYZ Agenda for First Merger Negotiations Committee Meeting

Time _____

Date _____

Location _____

1. Introduction of participants • Board members and CEOs introduce themselves	15 minutes	Consultant
2. Overview of organization ABC • History, funding, programs, major accomplishments	15 minutes	Executive
3. Overview of organization XYZ • History, funding, programs, major accomplishments	15 minutes	Executive
4. Review of desired outcomes and critical issues	25 minutes	Everyone
5. The options for a merger • An overview of all the ways to execute a merger	20 minutes	Consultant
6. Brainstorming the issues to be considered • What are all the issues and questions everyone in the room would need to have an answer to before voting on a recommendation to merge?	60 minutes	Everyone
7. Break	15 minutes	
8. Begin working through issues • Begin with any deal-breakers • Next work on governance, mission, and vision issues	90 minutes	Consultant
9. Scheduling future meetings • How much time do we need for homework prior to the next meeting?	15 minutes	Consultant

be the executive directors, since, as observed earlier, it is important that the negotiations be clearly labeled a board process. It is entirely appropriate for the committee cochairs to be the respective board chairs.

The first item on the agenda should be introductions of the committee members. In addition to name and any office held on the board, each board member should describe what he or she does for a living. This helps break the ice and humanizes the process.

After introductions, each executive director should provide a brief overview of his or her organization and distribute materials that can be taken home for more thorough review. This "dog and pony show" ensures that the negotiators at least share a common understanding of the organizations. It can also help build interest and excitement among the committee members, who may well be impressed by the other organization's operations, size, history, or political connections.

At this point the group should review the results of any assessment discussions that have taken place. Most important to discuss are each organization's desired outcomes and critical issues. Putting these on butcher paper, and leaving them up during the negotiations, can help keep them salient to people as the negotiations proceed.

It is important for the negotiators to have in mind at the outset the variety of ways in which the merger might be accomplished

Next, someone should give an overview of the options for executing a merger. This is a good role for a consultant to play. It is important for the negotiators to have in mind at the outset the variety of ways in which the merger might be accomplished. There is no need at this point to discuss which options might be preferred, only to make it clear that the form of the merger will follow the function deemed necessary by the committee. This step is essential at this early stage as it will broaden the negotiators' thinking about their options and may help to lessen their anxiety. Use Chapter 1, Forms of Merger, to prepare a presentation on the options for merger.

Next, the facilitator or committee chair leads a brainstorming session, asking, *"What are all the issues each of you would need to see resolved before you could cast a vote for or against a merger?"* An easy way to brainstorm is to write the issues raised by the negotiators onto separate sheets of butcher paper, each headed with one of the categories indicated in Exhibit 5, Typical Issues in Merger Negotiations (page 86). (These categories usually encompass all of the various issues raised in a merger process.) Exhibit 5 also includes examples of issues that commonly fall into each category, though it is by no means exhaustive. Keep this list nearby when brainstorming; the facilitator can use it to suggest items that the negotiators do not mention. Remember that there are no "bad" issues. What is important at this point is to get everyone's concerns out into the open. Once all the issues unique to your situation are framed, the group can begin working on each issue. This usually begins with governance issues, specifically with mission and vision.

Exhibit 5. Typical Issues in Merger Negotiations

Governance Issues	What is the mission of the new organization?
	What is our vision for the future? (How will things be better together?)
	Who will be on the merged board of directors?
	How many board members will there be?
	Who will be the officers in the first year?
	What committees will we have?
	How will we legally structure the merger?
	What will be the name and logo of the merged organization?
	What will be the role of our advisory board?
	What will be the effective date of the merger?
Financial Issues	Which accounting system will we use?
	Is the other group in debt?
	Will we need as many finance office staff?
	Will we need new software or hardware?
	How will our information system needs be met?
	What do the audits tell us about the organization's financial health?
	Is anyone suing the other group?
	Do both groups have adequate insurance, especially directors and officers coverage?
	What do our donors and funders think of the merger?
	Is there overlap in our donors or funders?
	What are the terms of our endowments relative to a merger or dissolution?
Human Resource Issues	Who will be the executive director?
	What will happen to the other senior staff?
	How do our pay and benefits stack up against the other group's?
	What personnel policies will we use?
	How will we maintain staff morale throughout the process?
	How will the presence of a union in one organization impact the other?
	What roles will each manager play in the new structure?
	Will anyone lose a job as a result of the merger; how will we handle severance?
	Will the two staffs work together well?
	For purposes of retirement vesting, will time worked in the other organization count?
	Will our carefully protected "at-will" employment status be weakened?
	Will our staff still get a pay differential for being bilingual?
Capital Issues	What will happen to our current office space when the lease is up?
	Do we need additional space? Where will we put all those people?
	What is the status of all properties occupied or controlled by each group?
	Do we have too many copiers? If we merge, can we get out of some copier leases?
	Which office will be headquarters?
	How will we address the other organization's deferred maintenance needs?

Programmatic Issues	Will all of our programs still be offered?
	Will we consolidate or close any program service sites?
	Do we tend to agree in our approach to programming?
	Can we do staff training jointly?
	Will programs be improved or expanded as a result of the merger?
Communication Issues	What should we tell our employees during the process?
	Should we issue a press release to inform the public?
	What opportunities for marketing will the merger create?
	If we don't merge, how will we end the discussions without a public relations disaster?
	If we don't merge, how do we know you won't use information against us?

Working through all of the issues raised will probably take several meetings, and may require homework in the interim periods. Take enough time to consider and discuss each issue raised, but at the same time the facilitator should keep the committee from getting bogged down over any one issue or debate. Keep in mind that the solution to a seemingly insurmountable challenge or disagreement may be something no one had previously considered. Be aware also of issues that are best left to staff's discretion post-merger. Be open-minded when negotiating, but also be mindful of your bottom-line concerns. Always remember what your ultimate goals are for the merger, and be creative in trying to craft an agreement that helps you reach those goals. Compromise willingly on peripheral issues but hold fast to issues essential to advancing your mission.

Minutes

After each meeting a recorder should collect the butcher paper, as well as his or her own written notes, and create a written summary of the meeting. We have found a particular type of meeting minutes most useful to merger discussions. These minutes differ markedly from those of the average board meeting. (For an example, see Exhibit 6, Sample Minutes for First Meeting, page 89.)

The first item, normally entitled *Summary of Issues and Agreements to Date,* consists of the brainstormed list of issues under their respective headings. After listing all the issues, go back and fill in any agreements the committee reached.

As you can see from the example (in which we have only filled in the "Governance" category), the minutes should include a complete list of the issues raised, whether a particular issue was actually considered at the meeting or simply deferred to a later time. In the space after those issues in which at least a tentative resolution has been reached, the minutes should include a written description of the agreements. Any issues the committee has not yet addressed are listed with the designation "not discussed."

The next section of the minutes, *Homework,* includes the tasks that committee members, staff, and consultants must complete prior to the next meeting. Homework assignments make it clear what must be done if the next meeting is to be productive.

The final section of the minutes is the agenda for the next meeting. Here it is important for the negotiators to agree in advance what will be tackled at the next meeting.

Create a Solid Foundation

The first meeting of the merger negotiations committee is critical. It sets the tone for the negotiations, begins developing relationships between the team of negotiators, lays out the issues to be addressed, and gives everyone a sense of how much work will be involved in getting to a decision. Successful completion of this meeting sends you well on your way to a successful merger negotiation process.

One of the benefits of this form of minute-taking is that it is a cumulative process. At the end of the second meeting you simply add to, adjust, and fill in additional blanks in the issues list from the previous meeting. As each successive set of minutes is issued, you may dispose of the previous set. By following this process, you will complete the negotiations with a cumulative set of minutes.

Dispensing with all but the most recent set of minutes prevents the confusion that can arise when a committee of ten tries to determine which of the eight previous sets of minutes contains just the item someone wanted to discuss. This problem is particularly nettlesome given that the agreements reached the first time an issue is discussed may change at a subsequent meeting, or at several subsequent meetings, in light of decisions related to other issues or reactions by either party's full board. A secondary benefit of this form of minute-taking is that it avoids the tendency, skewered so well in Brian O'Connell's *Board Overboard*, to record each participant's individual statements (see Resource List). This tiresome practice often makes it difficult to discern the important from the procedural or even the irrelevant.

A third substantial benefit to this form of minute-taking is that at the end of the negotiations process, your minutes, with a few additions and format changes, can be submitted to the boards as the draft merger agreement.

When you have discussed and resolved a sufficient number of issues to feel confident about your intention to move forward, it is time to undertake an essential, if somewhat daunting task: the due diligence process.

Due diligence process

Due diligence is the process by which confidential legal and financial information is exchanged, reviewed, and appraised by the parties. The essence of the due diligence process is an effort to make everyone on the negotiations committee, and by extension everyone on each board, as aware as a prudent board member can be of any liabilities the other party may bring to the merger. The desire is to create a "no surprises" situation. That is, if you've honestly performed "no surprises" due diligence in negotiations, no one can claim to be surprised when a balloon payment on a loan becomes due six months after the merger's effective date.

Exhibit 6. Sample Minutes for First Meeting

ABC/XYZ Merger Negotiations Committee
Minutes of Meeting of November 21

1. Summary of Issues and Agreements to Date

Governance Issues

What committees will we have - The merged organization will have the following committees: executive, finance, development, personnel, membership

How will we legally structure the merger   Not discussed

What will be the name of the merged organization - The committee proposes the following name for the corporation: ABC Community Center

What will be our new logo - Not discussed

2. Homework

- Everyone will draft ideal mission and vision statements for the new organization for discussion next time.

- Staff will complete a side-by-side comparison of all positions and salaries in the two organizations.

3. Next Meeting

Next Meeting Agenda
April 22, 4-7 PM
At the ABC offices
123 Main Street

1. Review of the previous meeting's minutes
2. Discussion of the mission and vision of the organization
3. Finish other governance issues
4. Begin discussion of personnel issues with salary comparisons

Often attorneys or consultants undertake the due diligence process on behalf of, and report their findings to, the merger negotiations committee. We recommend that the committee undertake the leadership of the process itself, relying on outside experts only as necessary. In this way the negotiators become intimately familiar with each other's operations. They can then provide more focused questions for any consultants or attorneys who are retained to conduct further analysis, saving time and money.

A substantial list of documents should be exchanged early in the negotiations process for review by each party. For a typical list, see Exhibit 7, Due Diligence Items to Be Exchanged, on the facing page. The exchanged documents can then either be reviewed by each organization's attorneys and consultants, or, more economically, by the negotiations committee itself, perhaps aided by the merger facilitation consultant. This process takes time. The document exchange should happen early in the process to allow adequate time for the parties to digest the packages (often several inches thick), formulate questions, and seek answers.

If the committee decides to undertake the due diligence process itself, a good way to proceed is to organize the due diligence meetings into financial, legal, regulatory, and personnel sections, and then invite relevant experts (such as each organization's accountant) to provide information at the appropriate point. Each section could be scheduled for a separate meeting, or, in a simpler situation, they could be linked together in a day-long series of discussions.

Choosing how to structure the merger

As you recall from Chapter 1, merger is a generic term for a type of partnership in which two or more corporations decide to become one. There are several ways to legally implement such a partnership. While it may not be possible to choose a specific method without legal advice, the negotiations committee should, at a minimum, consider and discuss the issue. Often the committee will be able to evaluate the options and choose a preferred one on its own, especially if the due diligence process was thorough enough to raise any issues that might be relevant. If not, the committee can prepare a list of questions, potential issues, and preferences for an attorney, who can use these to weigh the options and make a recommendation to the committee and the boards. In either case, an attorney should be consulted before any legal action is taken, both to review the choices made and ensure that they are appropriate and legal, and to highlight any special filing requirements in your state. Such legal review is discussed in more detail in Chapter 6.

Following is a brief description of the options for implementing merger, as well as some tips and worksheets designed to help you choose between them.

Exhibit 7. Due Diligence Items to Be Exchanged

Organizational Documents

- Articles of incorporation
- Bylaws
- Organizational chart
- Copies of any affiliation agreements, partnership agreements, or joint venture agreements in effect
- A list of all current officers and directors
- Conflict of interest statement
- Copies of board minutes from the last five years
- Tax documents
- IRS tax exemption letter
- State tax exemption letter
- Last three years' 990 submissions
- Copy of the most recent state tax filing
- Other federal and state tax records agreed upon

Insurance Documents

- A description of all insurance policies/coverages, copies of all policies
- Public liability, including automobiles
- Officers and directors
- Fire and extended coverage property
- Workers compensation
- Professional practice
- Volunteers coverage

Personnel Documents

- A listing of all current employees, their job descriptions, and their annual pay levels
- Copies of all employment contracts
- Copies of personnel policies
- Copies of all collective bargaining agreements
- A description of all employee benefit programs, including vendor contact information
- Copies of volunteer policies, including job descriptions and agreements

Finance / Funding

- Last three years' audited financial statements
- Accountant's management letter
- Most current financial statements
- The names and addresses of the organization's financial institutions
- A listing of all liabilities
- A schedule of all assets
- Copies of any loans or liens against any assets
- A statement confirming whether any interested party (board member, employee, their spouse or close relative) has an interest in any asset owned by the corporation
- A description of the terms, conditions, and status of all current grants and contracts
- A description of the terms, restrictions, and agreements for all restricted funds, including any endowment
- Fundraising program summary and any fundraising agreements

Capital / Real Estate

- Deeds
- Leases (for all buildings and equipment)
- Mortgages
- List of significant equipment and vehicles
- Zoning and use permits
- Other real estate records agreed upon

Other

- Copies of all operating licenses, accreditations, etc.
- Copies of marketing pieces and any other literature distributed to the public about the organization and its activities
- A statement describing any threatened or pending litigation or affirming that none exists
- A statement describing any threatened or pending government investigations

Outright merger

Chapter 1 outlined the three methods for implementing an outright merger. The first, "merger by dissolution into," involves dissolving one of the corporations (the disappearing corporation) into the other (the surviving corporation). The disappearing corporation thus leaves its assets and liabilities to the surviving corpora-

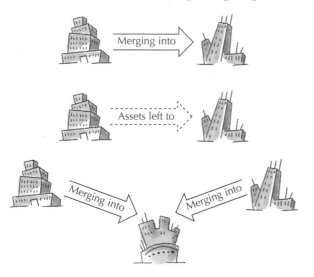

tion. The second method is to simply dissolve one corporation as if it were going out of business, and transfer its assets to the merger partner. The third, and most time-consuming, method involves dissolving both corporations into a new corporation, which must be created for that purpose.

Under either of the first two variations, a decision must be made about which corporation will survive and which will dissolve. This decision should be made on technical rather than emotional grounds. While this makes *logical* sense, emotions do often rise to the fore, and organizations often resist the idea of dissolving while their partner continues to exist as a legal entity. This often leads people to propose the third method of merging, even when there is no other pressing reason to go through the increased effort that would be

involved. There are ways to work around most people's concerns, however. The following example illustrates this:

> *Corporations "A" and "B" are considering a merger. While both parties agree that certain liability issues make it most desirable for "A" to dissolve into "B," "A" is reluctant to give up its name, to which it feels a great deal of attachment. "A" need not resist dissolution for this reason alone, however: the parties can agree to dissolve corporation "A," merge its assets and liabilities into corporation "B" and then change "B's" name to "A." In other words (and using a specific example) Neighborhood Community Services, Inc. could merge/dissolve into the Little Mites Child Care Center, and the board could then vote to change Little Mites' name to Neighborhood Community Services. The significance of the choice of corporate shell should be governed by practical, often financial concerns, not by ego. Moreover, name, choice of board members, and selection of the executive director have far greater influence over the organization's relative positions after merger than does choice of corporate shell.*

There are other factors to consider, as well. As illustrated in Chapter 1, it may or may not be a good idea to bring both parties' liabilities into the merged organization, and there may be possible future bequests to consider. Worksheet 18, Which Corporation Should Dissolve?, page 217, highlights some other issues that should be considered, and helps you decide among the various approaches. (Note that Worksheet 18 shows three organizations merging; the considerations are the same as for two organizations, our more often-used example.)

WORKSHEET 18 Which Corporation Should Dissolve?

Fill in the chart below, using check marks to indicate that a statement is true for a given organization.

	Corporation 1: **ABC Center**	Corporation 2: **GoodWorks**	Corporation 3: **XYZ Inc.**
The corporation has a license or certification that would be very difficult to obtain or transfer (e.g., FQHC – Federally Qualified Health Center).	X		X
The corporation has significant debt which must be repaid if it dissolves because the creditor is unwilling to transfer the obligation to a different entity.			
The corporation has a funding source that is unwilling to transfer the funding to a new entity.			
The corporation was created by statute and requires governmental action to dissolve.	X		
The corporation is a membership organization and the members will not approve the dissolution of the corporation.			

The more check marks an organization has under its name, the less likely it is that it should be the dissolving corporation. This worksheet should help make clear that the choice of who "survives" and who dissolves is not a matter of winning and losing but instead depends on practical considerations.

Based on the above, it appears that GoodWorks is the only organization of the three that can dissolve with impunity. Since ABC Center would have the hardest time dissolving, it looks like we should leave that as the corporate shell, and dissolve GoodWorks and XYZ Inc. into ABC Center. XYZ will then be able to function under ABC Center's FQHC certification.

Occasionally, Worksheet 18 will reveal that both corporations involved in a merger have reason to survive. In one case we know of, a governmental funder only allows $150,000 of a certain kind of funding per corporation. Each of two merging partners had that maximum amount. Thus, merging the corporations would entail the loss of $150,000 per year, every year.

In another situation one corporation had a Federally Qualified Health Center (FQHC) designation, very difficult if not impossible to obtain these days, while the other had $90,000 drawn on a line of credit and the bank said it would demand payment in full if the corporation dissolved.

In situations such as these it may be necessary to maintain two separate corporations. There are several ways to do this while still fulfilling the intent of the merger. The two corporations could effect an asset transfer, create a parent-subsidiary relationship, or opt for interlocking boards.

Asset transfer

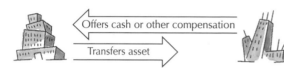

Asset transfers are transactions in which corporations remain separate, but some or all of the valuable assets of one corporation, which may include money and real property as well as a name or other intangibles, are "purchased" by the other. This purchase may be for cash, but is commonly for some other consideration.

When all or substantially all of a corporation's assets are acquired, this may trigger a review by the state authority responsible for nonprofits, typically the attorney general or the secretary of state. This review is usually required to ensure that the nonprofit's assets remain dedicated to their original charitable intent. Again, it is important that you obtain advice from an attorney who is familiar with the nonprofit code requirements in your state.

Asset transfers are sometimes written out as bills of sale, keeping the transaction simple. If a corporation disposes of all its assets to its merger partner in this way (and with the proper state review), it can still exist as a nonprofit corporation, albeit only a shell. If it then transacts less than $25,000 worth of business in a year, it is exempt from filing IRS Form 990, and the government will be perfectly content to let it lie dormant. It can then either be dissolved at a later date or resurrected when a need for a separate corporation arises. Tens (if not hundreds) of thousands of these shell nonprofits exist across America.

A remaining shell corporation may also be used as a receptacle for funds when funders are reluctant to transfer their contracts and grants to another entity. Once received, these funds can often be subcontracted, with the funder's permission, to the other organization, where all of the staff, payroll, and other activities are actually "housed."

It is important to note that if you decide to maintain two separate, active corporations, your merger will probably not realize substantial savings in the areas of insurance, payroll, accounting, audit, and other aspects of corporate systems. Many of these activities have threshold expenses (for example, it is difficult to obtain an audit of any organization for less than $2,500) and these would still be incurred by both corporations.

Important Note: All of the issues discussed in this section pertain only to the acquisition of a nonprofit's assets by another 501(c)(3) public charity. If the purchaser is a business, a private individual, an unincorporated nonprofit association, or any nonprofit or for-profit entity other than one with a 501(c)(3) IRS designation, a different and complex set of rules applies. If this description applies to your situation, stop and get legal advice before moving any further. On the other hand, if the acquiring entity is a 501(c)(3) and the assets belong to a business or an individual, the transaction is far simpler. You will still need to get legal advice, particularly if any party to the transaction is a board member, officer, employee, or relative of the same at the nonprofit.

Worksheet 19, Transferring Assets, page 219, helps you plan an asset transfer.

WORKSHEET 19   Transferring Assets

Indicate which assets your corporation wishes to transfer (or acquire), and their approximate value. Each asset may be exchanged for cash, or for an agreement to preserve and protect it, or for further consideration. Fill in the type of exchange under the heading "Method of payment."

Note: if the transferring 501(c)(3) corporation is distributing all or substantially all of its assets, or if the sale is to anything but another public charity (regardless of the size of the sale), stop and seek legal counsel before you proceed. These transactions, if handled improperly, can bring serious negative tax consequences, including the payment of taxes and penalties or the possible loss of the organization's tax exemption.

Name of organization *from* which these assets would be transferred: **Our City Ballet**

Name of organization *to* which these assets would be transferred: **Shows Unlimited**

Description of asset	Approximate value	Method of payment
Sets and costumes for 3 shows	$2.5 million	Agree to conserve asset
Archives of 50 years of experience	$75,000	Agree to curate
2 contracts for recording	$400,000	Agree to use funds to stage a new ballet
TOTAL:	$2,975,000	

Interlocking boards

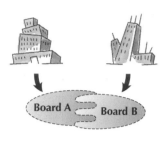

Two organizations may desire to merge, but for technical reasons need to keep the two corporations alive for at least some time into the future. The quickest and easiest way to "merge" two such nonprofits is to create interlocking boards. In other words, the parties reconfigure their boards so that the same group of individuals makes up both boards. There are still two separate corporations, but the boards have the same membership.

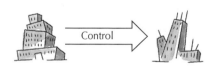

There are advantages to creating interlocking boards. Because they are easy to create and do not require any legal paperwork or filings, they make a good intermediary step for organizations waiting for the legal process of a full merger to run its course. They allow for unified control of the organizations in the short term, which can facilitate planning and implementation efforts.

As described in Chapter 1, however, interlocking boards, while easily and quickly accomplished, create only loosely coupled entities. There are costs associated with keeping two separate organizations and there may be "drift" in board membership if they are maintained for a long period of time. It is a great way to expedite the merger process and represents the best of the spirit of a merger, but should not be the first choice for a long-term arrangement.

One other potential concern must be noted. While the creation of interlocking boards may accomplish many of your goals, as described above, it may also cause the two corporations to be viewed as one by the IRS for reporting purposes. It will also likely create joint liability for one another's actions. Again, legal counsel should be consulted with regard to your particular situation.

Worksheet 20, Creating Interlocking Boards, pages 221–222, helps you design the new interlocking boards structure.

Parent-subsidiary relationships

One way to maintain two separate corporations while preventing the possibility of drifting board membership—a possible outcome of interlocking boards—is to create the nonprofit equivalent of a parent-subsidiary relationship. As described in Chapter 1, this is most often accomplished by making one organization into a membership corporation and stipulating that its only member is the other organization. This is done by changing the bylaws of the organization designated as the subsidiary. The updated bylaws specify that the organization is a membership corporation (pursuant to the law in your state) and has only one member. It names the other corporation as that member. It should also state in the appropriate bylaws section (usually "Election of Directors") that the board of directors is elected by the membership (which of course is the other organization).

WORKSHEET 20   Creating Interlocking Boards

Use this worksheet to help you design an interlocking board. As a first step, list the names of all current members of each board of directors.

Org Name: **ABC for the Environment**   Org Name: **Save the XYZ**

	ABC for the Environment		Save the XYZ
1.	Cesar C.	1.	Rutherford H.
2.	Tom J.	2.	Simon B.
3.	Mario C.	3.	Omar S.
4.	Sandy K.	4.	Bruce L.
5.	Kermit F.	5.	Olivia R.
6.	Marie C.	6.	Jane G.
7.	Thomas E.	7.	Pierre S.
8.	John G.	8.	Margaret M.
9.	Susan A.	9.	Mary P.
10.	David Ben G.	10.	Fidel C.
11.	Beatrix P.	11.	James M.
12.	Alexander B.	12.	
13.	Nancy D.	13.	

Now determine how many slots the newly constituted boards will have. In order to avoid creating an unwieldy board you may need to reduce the total number of board slots. For example, if there are 24 board members, you may want to create interlocking boards with a total of 12 members, 6 from each group. List below the names of those board members who will continue on to serve as members of the boards of both organizations. At their respective board meetings, ask each organization to elect this group as its board.

Board of *Both* Organizations

1.	Cesar C.	5.	Beatrix P.	9.	James M.
2.	Tom J.	6.	Susan A.	10.	Jane G.
3.	Marie C.	7.	Rutherford H.	11.	Pierre S.
4.	Thomas E.	8.	Simon B.	12.	Margaret M.

Since both corporations remain intact, the decision as to which organization is the parent and which the subsidiary is not so technical as in the case of a merger by dissolution. Here, the reasons for placing one group "over" the other in the corporate hierarchy relate most directly to power and control: who has it and how it will be shared. Of course, if one organization is a larger, umbrella organization comprised of several operating units and the other is a single-purpose organization, it would probably make sense to place the latter under the former's umbrella. Or, if one organization has a far more sophisticated management structure and systems, it might make sense to place this entity as the parent.

The parent, as the sole member of the subsidiary, elects the subsidiary's board at the latter's annual meeting. It matters less here than in the case of interlocking boards that the two boards have identical membership, since the parent always maintains the right to remove the board of the subsidiary. When electing the board, the parent has, essentially, four choices:

1. It may elect its own entire board as the subsidiary's board, creating, in essence, interlocking boards.

2. It may elect a subset of its board to serve as the subsidiary's board if it wishes the subsidiary to have a smaller board.

3. It may choose a group of non-board members—for example, its senior managers—to serve as the subsidiary's board.

4. It may elect some representatives by either method two or three above, and then allow that core board to freely choose some number of additional board members. (In this case it is important that every board member, however recruited, understands that the parent organization's board ultimately elects him or her.)

An easier way to accomplish the same ends, avoiding the need to reformulate one of the corporations as a membership corporation, was suggested by William Staley, a Los Angeles-based nonprofit attorney. Here, one corporation changes its bylaws to read that its board of directors is elected by the other corporation. It further amends its bylaws to state that it cannot in the future amend its bylaws without the consent of the other corporation. These moves give the same effective control to the parent corporation as the slightly more involved method suggested above.

As with interlocking boards, the control exercised by one organization over another may cause the IRS to view the corporations as one organization for reporting purposes.

Making the choice

The negotiations committee should discuss the options and considerations outlined above, and record any preferences and/or recommendations in the minutes, along with the other agreements it reaches during the negotiations process.

Decision Tree 3 on this page can help in determining which form of merger is most appropriate. If the committee is not sure which method is best, and neither organization has a preference, the decision can be left until after the individual boards approve the committee's overall recommendation to merge. At that point a lawyer will be needed to review the proposed merger agreement, provide legal feedback, and file the appropriate paperwork; he or she can also advise the boards with regard to the most appropriate method of merger. This legal role is discussed in more detail in Chapter 6.

Decision Tree 3. What Form of Merger Should We Consider?

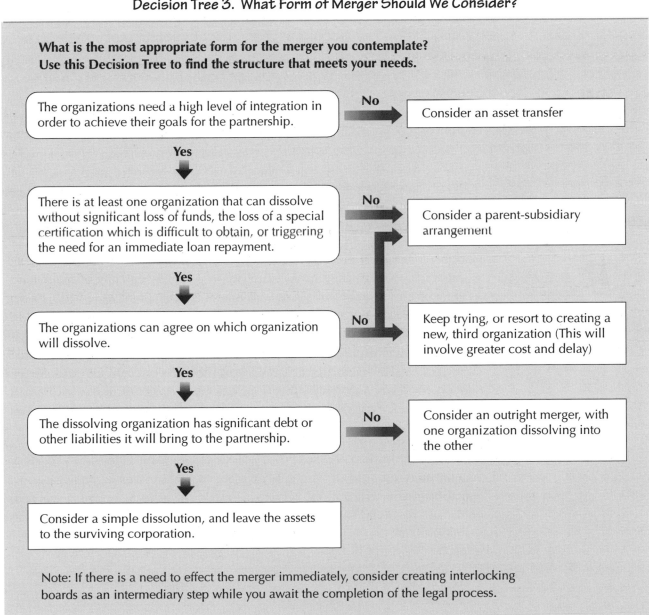

What is the most appropriate form for the merger you contemplate? Use this Decision Tree to find the structure that meets your needs.

The organizations need a high level of integration in order to achieve their goals for the partnership. — **No** → Consider an asset transfer

Yes

There is at least one organization that can dissolve without significant loss of funds, the loss of a special certification which is difficult to obtain, or triggering the need for an immediate loan repayment. — **No** → Consider a parent-subsidiary arrangement

Yes

The organizations can agree on which organization will dissolve. — **No** → Keep trying, or resort to creating a new, third organization (This will involve greater cost and delay)

Yes

The dissolving organization has significant debt or other liabilities it will bring to the partnership. — **No** → Consider an outright merger, with one organization dissolving into the other

Yes

Consider a simple dissolution, and leave the assets to the surviving corporation.

Note: If there is a need to effect the merger immediately, consider creating interlocking boards as an intermediary step while you await the completion of the legal process.

Communications and rumor control

It is tempting to say there is no point to trying to keep merger negotiations confidential. Once the concept gets beyond a small group of leaders, word of it will spread like wildfire. One board member we know returned home from a board meeting where the possibility of merging with another organization was discussed for the first time to find a message on her answering machine from a donor asking if the organization "was being taken over." Scary news travels fast and gets distorted even faster.

No matter how hard you try to keep it quiet, or to inform interested parties of the facts, experience tells us that the following rumors will be floating around your organization:

1) We are going out of business.

2) We are being gobbled up in a hostile takeover.

The persistence of these rumors frustrates negotiators who are doing everything in their power to keep everyone informed. As one staff member from an organization just beginning negotiations told me, "I keep asking what's going on and all management will tell me is that they don't know." Unfortunately, management's answer is probably honest. Early in the process there are far more questions than answers, and saying "I don't know" is probably the most honest response possible. Still, it does little to calm the fears of the staff, or for that matter the community.

The best one can do under these circumstances is to communicate forthrightly and often. After each meeting of the negotiations committee a copy of the minutes should be posted at each organization's offices, so that all may see what is being discussed. Of course, confidential issues such as those involving collective bargaining, salaries, and the choice of executive director, should first be edited out of the public copy of the minutes. Nonetheless, the remaining issues are of great interest to staff. A similarly edited copy of the minutes could be distributed to donors, foundation program officers, or others who have expressed an interest. The full board of each organization should, of course, receive an unabridged copy of the minutes.

Some board members and executives believe the negotiations must be kept confidential until completed. This is difficult and is usually unnecessary. If negotiations are to be held in secret, the full boards, at least, must be kept informed. Negotiators must also recognize that if the secret gets out, it will look very bad.

Another way to enhance communication during the negotiations process is through direct face-to-face meetings. While sometimes volatile, staff meetings are often useful in this regard. Such meetings are more productive if preceded by a survey of staff views of the potential merger. (See Pre-Merger Staff Survey, page 215, for an example.) Tabulate the results of both organizations' responses to the survey, include a sample of responses to the open-ended questions, and then share the results with staff at each nonprofit through facilitated discussions. In one pre-merger situation, where the staff of each nonprofit had very similar, and very negative, views of one another, sharing the survey results helped bring some perspective to both parties. After reviewing the summary one person remarked, "You mean they think we're as bad as we think they are?"

Regularly scheduled board meetings occurring during the course of the negotiations should include as a standing item a progress report from the organization's delegation to the merger negotiations committee. This is an opportunity for the committee to gain feedback from the larger board and to test whether it is on the right track, negotiating an arrangement the board will accept.

Occasionally outsiders such as donors, community leaders, or (very rarely) the press will call for an update, or to check out a wild story about the organization's rumored demise. For just these situations, the negotiations committee (or perhaps the development or communications staff of either organization) should craft a brief, factual statement that both organizations can use as a template in their discussions with the public. An example of such a statement would be:

> *"ABC has entered into negotiations with XYZ to see if it makes sense for us to join forces. While it is too early to speculate on the outcome, a positive working relationship has been established and a committee representing both organizations is working diligently on the many issues involved."*

This factual statement will help to buy some time. After such a statement is crafted, it must be approved for distribution by both boards. Once approval is granted, every negotiator, board member, and manager in both organizations should be handed a copy and told that this—and this alone—is what they are authorized to say in response to any inquiries on the topic.

If, upon completion of the negotiations, the merger is approved by both organizations, communications will shift from a focus on rumor control to an emphasis on celebration. Press releases, a convening of funders, open houses, and letters to the editor should all be considered part of a celebration strategy, which should be coordinated between the two organizations. There is a great (if short-lived) potential for positive public response to a merger, and this should be taken advantage of as quickly as possible.

Truth Is the Best Policy

The truth, absent any confidential or embarrassing information, is usually the best public relations for your organization, especially for this effort.

If the negotiations end in a decision *not* to move ahead with a merger, the two organizations should issue a joint statement, each praising the good-faith efforts of the other organization and wishing them luck in the future. This statement should be approved by the respective boards of directors and issued simultaneously. It should also replace the "status report" board members and managers were asked to use in prior communications. A sample statement might say:

"ABC and XYZ have concluded that at this time it is not in the best interest of either the organizations, their clients, or the advancement of their missions to affiliate. Throughout the negotiations we have been impressed by each other's honesty, openness, and dedication to (fill in the generic mission, such as "Helping children in our community"). While we will not be moving forward with the affiliation, we will remain in communication, working together toward a brighter future for our community."

Step 3: Write and Give Proposed Agreement to the Board

Early in the negotiations process the committee should be advised that it has a very wide berth in which to navigate. It may develop the partnership in whatever way appears to offer the greatest advantage to the organizations. Ironically, this relative freedom is possible because the committee has no authority to implement its recommendations. This right is reserved for the boards of directors of the respective organizations and, in the case of membership organizations, for the membership itself. Thus, at the point that the negotiations committee comes to agreement, the following questions arise:

1) What, exactly, have we agreed to?

2) What do we do now?

The first question can be answered by reviewing the cumulative minutes of the committee's meetings. At the conclusion of the negotiations the minutes should reflect all the agreements reached by the negotiators. If the process was well-conceived and executed, it will have addressed all the major concerns of the negotiators. Often, not every issue raised in the initial brainstorming exercise must be addressed before an agreement is reached. The negotiators may reach the "tipping point" at which enough of the major issues have been resolved, and they are confident the remaining issues can be worked out after the merger decision. Appendix A has a sample set of final minutes from a completed negotiation. You can study this to see how the minutes reflect the discussions and decisions made about each issue in the merger.

Despite having addressed all the reasons why a merger might or might not be a good idea, it is often at this point that a kind of buyer's remorse sets in: *"We know we can do it, we know what it will look like if we do it, but do we REALLY want to do it?"* To remedy this situation, return to the list of motivators and desired outcomes. If these are still applicable and compelling, and if it looks like the negotiated partnership will help to accomplish them, then the committee will most likely overcome its reluctance and vote to move ahead.

It is important to recognize the point at which the negotiators have completed their charge: when they have either negotiated the terms of a deal or determined that they cannot in good conscience recommend a merger. At this point, the committee needs to stop its meetings and bring its recommendation back to the individual boards. Occasionally, the momentum of the committee's work and the relationships that have developed will cause the negotiators to plan to continue meeting to discuss strategy and implementation after they have concluded the negotiations. *This temptation should be avoided.* The committee must disband and return with its recommendation to the boards, which alone have authority to act and to implement. This is not to say that the committee will not be called back into existence to iron out emerging problems or to oversee implementation. At this stage, however, the next move belongs to the two boards, not to the negotiators.

Since the committee has no formal authority, its process for approving the draft merger agreement will likely be informal. Often the committee will act by consensus. If this is not possible, each delegation must decide for itself what level of agreement it needs in order to return to its board with a positive recommendation. For example, one group's delegation may feel it needs unanimous support, while another may feel that a two-thirds majority is good enough.

If a decision to return a positive recommendation is reached by both delegations, the written agreement can be spruced up, a preface added, and the document submitted to the boards for their consideration. If one or both delegations to the negotiations committee decide not to move forward there are two choices: return to negotiations, perhaps by asking the respective boards to appoint a couple of additional negotiators to bring in a fresh perspective, or consider the matter dead.

This is an especially critical point in the process. All the chips are on the table, including, possibly, executive director positions, board seats, endowments, and the prestige of individuals and organizations. It is important to expedite this stage, as a long delay allows things to spin out of control. Anxieties that have mounted throughout the process may reach a critical stage, with potentially explosive results. Skillful navigation of the decision-making process at the merger negotiations committee level is essential to keeping the process on track.

Step 4: Approve or Reject the Agreement

Each board member should receive a copy of the proposed agreement well in advance of the board meeting at which it will be addressed. Board members must be given time to review the document, which could be lengthy and may contain some complex terms.

Often it is useful for the lead negotiators from each organization (with the consultant, if one is used) to make a joint presentation at both board meetings where the matter will be considered. After the presentation, and a suitable interval for questions, the negotiator who is not a member of the board currently meeting should leave, allowing the deliberations to proceed.

The decision to merge (or not) may well be difficult to reach. Often feelings run deep. Occasionally, board members who have been quiet throughout the process—despite every effort to have a full airing of concerns—wait until this moment to voice a strong objection, raise a concern no one has considered, or even slander members of the other board or staff. It is important to hear every voice, but also to keep the process on track. Here again, an experienced consultant can be useful.

The question before the board at this stage is usually one of intent. There are no legal papers at the meeting, and no legal action must be taken. The board is asked to vote on a resolution such as one of the following:

> *"The executive director is directed to engage legal counsel in order to cause a merger between our corporation and XYZ."*

> *"The board commits the corporation to a legal merger with XYZ at the earliest date."*

> *"The executive director is instructed to acquire the following assets of XYZ: its archives, its name, and its programs, in exchange for the nonmonetary consideration and assurances described in the proposed merger agreement before us today."*

Ideally, the two boards meet simultaneously. However, in the real world, this ideal is seldom attainable. The next best option is for the boards to meet in close chronological proximity. Obviously, if the first board votes "no," the second board has just received the gift of a great deal of free time at its next meeting. Sometimes, it is clear to the negotiators that one board will be more reluctant than the other to approve the merger. In this case it is often wise to schedule the meetings so that the reluctant board meets first. This spares the other organization the possible embarrassment of being "left at the altar," having approved the merger, only to find that the other group refuses the deal.

It is essential that throughout the time the boards are considering the agreement the two board chairs stay in close communication. It is possible, for example, that defecting parties of board members may try to scuttle the deal, perhaps aided by an executive director who fears for his or her job. Communication between the groups is critical to recognizing and dealing with any such problems.

Take Time to Make the Right Decision

If the board is conflicted over the decision, it may also feel pressure to decide the issue at once, based on what it knows today. The board should resist that temptation. Instead, it should try to agree on what the sticking points are. Those sticking points should then be taken back to the potential partner for further negotiation.

Chapter Summary

Once two (or more) parties have identified a potential merger opportunity, each board of directors should approve a resolution to enter into good-faith negotiations with the other party. A joint merger negotiations committee should be formed, and a facilitator (or pair of facilitators, if board members are filling that role) chosen.

This committee should meet regularly to articulate and work through all of the issues that each party would like to see addressed before they feel comfortable making a final decision for or against a merger. As part of the committee's work, the two parties should undertake a due diligence process.

There are several ways to legally accomplish a merger, and the negotiations committee should consider and discuss the issue as part of its process. Legal advice should always be sought before a final decision is made, however.

The members of the merger negotiations committee should communicate regularly with their boards and management teams throughout the entire negotiations process, so as to keep board members informed and also to keep rumors to a minimum. Minutes should be kept and updated at each meeting. Once the committee reaches agreement on what course of action to recommend to the boards of directors, negotiators can reformat the final set of minutes into a proposed merger agreement. This agreement and the committee's recommendation can then be taken back to each board for discussion and a vote. While the merger negotiations committee has an important role in crafting the deal, it has no ultimate authority. This is left to the boards, which must vote to approve and move forward with any merger. Membership organizations, such as professional associations, often will have to go the further step of seeking approval of their members. The bylaws of a membership organization will stipulate the voting rights of members. These may entail the right to approve the merger or dissolution of the corporation.

10 Most Common Merger Mistakes

1. Diving into merger discussions without board approval
2. Beginning negotiations without understanding what you want to get out of the process
3. Assuming a superior attitude toward your potential partner
4. Withholding potentially embarrassing information from your partner
5. Breaking the confidentiality of the process, such as by talking to the press
6. Adding negotiators after the process has begun
7. Allowing the process to drag on too long
8. Not keeping your staff adequately informed of developments
9. Not communicating with the board throughout the negotiation process
10. Not getting competent nonprofit legal counsel

Case Studies

Stop HIV and Contra SIDA

The exploration committees for Stop HIV and Contra SIDA got together a week after the October board meetings to exchange and review all the documents they had accumulated throughout their individual exploration efforts. Antonio, the Contra SIDA chair, summarized the feelings of the group. "Though restructuring at this level will very likely involve difficulty and conflict, the evidence indicates that we are excellent candidates for a merger."

Byron, a veteran Stop HIV board member, concurred. "Our analysis shows that the potential rewards to our clients outweighs any difficulties we may encounter in attempting to merge." With that, the groups unanimously voted to recommend that their respective boards begin merger negotiations. They also recommended that

In a nutshell...

Stop HIV and Contra SIDA

Understanding the difficult tasks ahead of them, both boards authorized merger negotiations and appointed a negotiations committee. Surveys of staffs' attitudes about a merger were completed and analyzed. The negotiations committee discussed and resolved issues, completed the due diligence requirements, and recommended the board proceed to merge. They also recommended Carmen be named executive director.

the executive directors organize a joint meeting of the two boards for November, where the exploration committees could present their findings and where any other questions could be answered before the formal decision to enter into negotiations was made.

Carmen and Mary did as the committees requested, and at the November joint meeting the two boards informally resolved to enter into good-faith negotiations with each other. At their next regular board meetings, each board approved negotiations commitment resolutions and appointed the members of the exploration committees as members of the joint negotiations committee. In addition, they appointed the two board chairs, Julie and Antonio, as cofacilitators of the negotiation process.

The negotiations committee set up its initial meeting later in the month. In preparation, they asked the agencies' auditors and accountants, a real estate agent, both personnel directors, and both executive directors to begin gathering and analyzing due diligence information. Binders containing those documents were given to each person on the negotiations committee a week in advance of the first meeting.

In the meantime, the two executive directors surveyed their staffs' attitudes about a merger. The survey revealed that both staffs were agreeable to the idea, but wanted to learn more about the benefits before moving forward. In response to this, the two executive directors called a joint staff meeting in which they had the two board chairs describe their visions for the merger. The executive directors themselves took part in this presentation. After an exhaustive question-and-answer period, the executive directors repeated the survey. The results were much more favorable than those of the first survey. This gave the boards and executive directors greater confidence about the merger.

At the first negotiation meeting, the committee agreed to meet for two hours every other week until they had worked out all the issues surrounding the merger. The committee met five times to discuss program autonomy, composition of the new board, programmatic focus, differences in philosophy, executive director selection, location and building questions, and systems integration challenges. Antonio facilitated the process while Julie, the Stop HIV chair, sent accurate, timely minutes and notices to all committee members and kept the boards and staffs abreast of the committee's progress. By the fifth negotiations committee meeting, in mid-February, the group had discussed and resolved all of their issues and was ready to make a positive recommendation to the Contra SIDA and Stop HIV boards.

The due diligence meeting, which took place in late January, lasted four hours. At the end of the meeting, those attending drafted a statement on their findings. The statement declared that both organizations were in reasonably good financial health; that they found no hidden liabilities; that both corporations were in apparent good standing with the IRS and other regulatory agencies; and that, as far as the committee could see, neither party need concern itself with unexpected surprises in these areas.

The Contra SIDA and Stop HIV boards each met during the last week in February to receive the recommendations from the merger negotiations committee. The committee presented its final set of meeting minutes, redrafted as a proposed merger agreement, and reviewed the report issued by the due diligence task force. At the end of their half-hour presentation, they recommended that Contra SIDA and Stop HIV merge into one corporation. They also recommended that the new entity offer the position of executive director to the current Contra SIDA executive director.

After some discussion and minor revision of the documents presented, each board considered the following motion: "The board directs its executive director to engage legal counsel and related services to effect a merger between Contra SIDA and Stop HIV; and the board appoints a joint hiring committee to negotiate staff personnel issues raised by the merger." Both boards voted unanimously to accept the motions on the floor, thus paving the way for the two organizations to become one.

Community Arts Center and Museum of Art and Culture

After initial discussions, the boards of Museum of Art and Culture and Community Arts Center decided to move forward with good-faith negotiations. Each board selected a committee of four to represent them on the merger negotiations committee. Together the group members hired a consultant, Sara Tyler, to facilitate the process.

At the first meeting Sara led the committee through a discussion of what each organization did, what they were most proud of, and what they hoped to accomplish through a merger. She also had the group agree on a brief statement to answer inquiries from outsiders during the negotiation period. "You must present the same message—that you have entered into negotiations with each other to see if it makes sense for you to join forces in some way, and that you are enjoying the opportunity to work together to answer this question." She then described the options for merging and explained that it was not necessary to pick a precise legal form until later in the process.

Next the group brainstormed answers to the question "What are all the issues each of you would need to see resolved before you could cast a vote for or against a merger?" Before they were done there were over a dozen pieces of butcher paper lining the walls of the meeting room.

"This looks daunting," said Jack Cox of the Museum of Art and Culture with a sigh. "How are we ever going to come to agreement on all of these things?"

Sara was reassuring. "Think of it as a well-defined puzzle. We'll just keep moving down the list of issues until we get to the end. And we *will* get there!" During a break Sara organized the lists by categories, and found a great deal of overlap in the issues. There were really not as many individual issues as it first appeared.

In a nutshell...

Community Arts Center and Museum of Art and Culture

The boards approved negotiations and selected a committee to implement the process. The committee hired a consultant to facilitate their work. They began with deal-breaker issues, critical outcomes, and strategic focus. Rumors of pay cuts needed to be addressed and resolved; the incident actually lessened concerns about a merger. On the recommendation of the negotiation committee, the boards voted to merge.

Sara suggested that the group first define any deal-breaker issues and begin the discussions with those. Cameron Bose from Community Arts Center was the first to jump forward. "We want to be able to keep our focus on local artists. They *need* a forum, and the community is enriched by the exposure to their work that we provide."

Deidre Abelman spoke up for Museum of Art and Culture. "Your connection to the local community is an asset, and we would want you to keep that—it's what makes you strong. But *we* need to be assured that you will also work to promote more mainstream and high-profile exhibits. We also have a good reputation, and we can't have half our organization promoting local works at the expense of that. We need to present a united front in support of *all* art."

Over the next hour the group discussed its views on what was, in essence, a question of strategic focus. They discovered quite a bit of mutual respect. Jack Cox raised the question of resistant board members, saying that there were a few people on his board who thought that Community Arts Center's art was too "out there." Community Arts Center responded that they knew of at least a few patrons who actively supported both organizations and who might talk to Museum of Art and Culture's board.

"If your board members can see that people similar to them, who value 'mainstream' and better-known art like they do, also appreciate the kind of art we showcase, maybe they will feel better," suggested Alexandra Ryan of Community Arts Center. She agreed to work with Jackie to arrange for such a presentation at Museum of Art and Culture's next board meeting.

Over the course of the next three meetings the negotiations committee continued to work through the master list of issues. After each meeting Sara forwarded each of the negotiators a copy of the updated meeting minutes, summarizing the committee agreements to date. Committee members, in turn, shared these with their boards at regular board meetings, and the executive directors had regular staff meetings at their organizations to keep the staffs informed of what was going on. Once it appeared that it might be possible to reach an agreement on terms for a merger, the groups formed two subcommittees to focus on the due diligence process. These subcommittees found no apparent red flags, but noted that the terms of Museum of Art and Culture's endowment meant that it could not be the dissolving corporation when it came time to merge. Community Arts Center was uncomfortable with this at first, but understood the logic and agreed under the condition that the educational programs of the merged organizations could still operate under the name "Community Arts Center," and that all materials and public statements would include both organizations' names for at least the next two years.

In the midst of negotiations, Community Arts Center staff heard a rumor that Museum of Art and Culture had cut everyone's pay several years back, and had abruptly stopped offering its art appreciation classes for youth only six months after they had begun, firing everyone involved. The rumor spread quickly. One art instructor stormed out of a Community Arts Center staff meeting declaring, "I'll go to the papers if I need to! We can't work in such horrible conditions. How do we know they won't fire *us* if we merge?"

Marie, the executive director of Community Arts Center, quickly reassured the angry staff person that she would find out what happened, and that the merger negotiations committee would not agree to a process that resulted in pay cuts or firing of people who she agreed were clearly valuable to Community Arts Center's programming. She also made it clear to him that he needed to keep his concerns "in house." Marie then contacted Ron to get the real story. Ron confirmed what he knew with several board members, and then suggested two board members attend a Community Arts Center staff meeting and explain what had happened. In reality, there *was* a pay cut seven years before. It followed a huge cut in government funding. When the museum board realized it could not pay for its current year budget without making up that funding or severely cutting costs, the board called an all-staff meeting and made two proposals. Either four staff people could be laid off, or everyone in the organization (including management) could take a 10 percent pay cut for three months or until alternate funding was secured. Everyone agreed to the short-term pay cut, and at the end of three months everyone's pay was returned to its normal level. By explaining this directly to Community Arts Center's staff, and showing them that it was an organizational decision that was meant to *save* jobs in the face of a funding crisis, Museum of Art and Culture was able to alleviate Community Arts Center's fears and show that they shared Community Arts Center's commitment to its employees.

As it turned out, the "firings" never actually happened. Several years after the temporary pay cuts, when it became clear that its art appreciation classes for youth were not attracting enough people, the classes were canceled. The teachers were not let go, however, but moved to other departments within the museum.

Community Arts Center employees were reassured after their meeting with the Museum of Art and Culture board members. The whole incident, while trying, actually advanced the discussion because Community Arts Center's staff were treated with respect and honesty, reducing their concerns about the merger.

After four months of meetings and back-and-forth communication with each organization's constituencies, the merger negotiations committee approved a resolution recommending that the two organizations merge. Sara then used the final set of meeting minutes to draft a merger agreement. Each member of each board was sent a copy of the agreement, and board meetings for the final vote were scheduled for the last week of that month.

There were no surprises at those meetings, as communication had been frequent and thorough beforehand. In the end Peter Banks, from Museum of Art and Culture, was the only casualty. While he grudgingly agreed that the merger was probably in the best interests of both organizations (it helped that he had heard from several donors whom he knew and liked), he did not feel he could fairly represent the interests of the merged organization as a board member, and asked to step down. The rest of the board thanked him for his honesty, and reminded each other that in fact, five of them were stepping down as part of the merger agreement. Ten of Museum of Art and Culture's fifteen board members were going to join ten of Community Arts Center's fourteen board members to form the new board. With that, the Museum of Art and Culture board unanimously approved a motion to proceed with the merger. Four days later Community Arts Center's board voted to do the same thing. The organizations were going to merge!

CHAPTER 6

Implementation

Once the terms of the partnership are agreed upon,
how do you make the merger a reality?

ONCE a decision to merge has been reached and the boards have acted to approve it, what next? Although it may feel as if the organizations have finally scaled the mountain and can now take a well-deserved rest, a better analogy would be that they have just crested the top of a large hill and only now, with that barrier removed, can they see the even bigger climb to the summit looming ahead in the distance.

Implementation is in some ways straightforward: you file the appropriate papers, wait the necessary time, and you are merged. On the other hand, integration of people and processes in order to make real all of the previous discussions can be trying, conflict-laden, and in some cases may seem all but impossible.

Volumes could be written on managing the changes that occur when organizations merge. This chapter highlights the major issues for implementation. It is not a full treatment of the subject, which would merit its own book. Our desire here is simply to make the reader aware of the issues to be faced, and to suggest some general strategies. Remember, just as the fears and legitimate self-interests of the people affected by the merger can derail the negotiations process, so too can they impact the implementation phase. In fact the organizations' people—board members and staff in particular—can make the integration of the two organizations either far easier or a living hell.

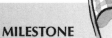

MILESTONE

The approval of an agreement to merge is a major achievement. Although there is still much to do before the merger can fairly be called a success, take the time now to celebrate, at least in-house. You may not be ready yet for a big public announcement and celebration, but the boards can hold an informal reception, and the staffs can sponsor open houses for each other. These or similar low-key celebrations can help mark an important milestone.

Pay serious attention to the cultural differences between the two organizations and respect the "way things have always been done" by your partner. This is not to say that you cannot change anything. However, a cavalier attitude, scoffing at a less sophisticated system or staff, or an assumption that your organization's way of doing things will be the merged way of doing things can make a tense situation worse. Listen to your colleagues—for that is what they are now—and always choose the most functional way of doing things, even if it requires change on your part.

Implementation versus Integration

There are three phases to a completed merger process. The first phase, Negotiation, begins at the point where two or more organizations decide to explore a possible merger together, and pass board resolutions to begin negotiations. It ends when both boards (or all boards, if there are more than two parties) vote either to move forward with the merger or to cease negotiations.

Merger Stages	
Phase 1 Negotiation	From intent to decision
Phase 2 Implementation	From decision to legal reality
Phase 3 Integration	Making the orga- nizations into one

The second phase can be called Implementation; it is the legal, practical process of bringing the merging organizations together. It involves hiring an attorney to review the proposed agreement, offer any needed advice with regard to the legal method of implementation, and file the necessary papers to make the merger happen. It is relatively straightforward in and of itself.

The third phase—Integration—is the most complex and time-consuming of the three phases. It involves the integration of governance, management, staff, and systems. It can take years to fully integrate merging organizations.

Time frame for implementation

If a merger is executed by the creation of either interlocking boards or a parent-subsidiary relationship, the time frame for implementation is very short. Often it may take each board only one meeting to act on the recommendation of the merger negotiations committee, and thus effect the merger. The two exceptions to this situation are the organization whose bylaws state that no changes can be made to the bylaws without a hearing of the changes in one meeting and then taking action the next; and the organization which has corporate members (members that elect the board). Even in these cases, two meetings are all that is required, assuming the members are agreeable to the merger.

Remember, all that needs to be done to create interlocking boards is to arrange board membership so that both boards are comprised of the same people. If you are creating a parent-subsidiary relationship, you need to effect a bylaws change to make one of the groups a membership organization with the other named as sole member, or to provide that one organization's board elects the board of the other organization.

If the merger is to be accomplished by the dissolution of one corporation, the responsible state body (Secretary of State, Corporations Secretary, or Attorney General) will have appropriate papers for filing. If your state also requires tax clearance, this step must be gained first. These processes can take several months.

If your process involves a transfer of assets that are a relatively small portion of the nonprofit's total assets (for example, an arts program that is just one of hundreds of departments at a major university) *and* the transfer is to another 501(c)(3) public charity, then the transaction can be carried out as quickly as your attorney can draw up the papers. If the acquisition involves substantially all of the assets of the nonprofit, or if the transfer is to anything but a public charity, then you will need state approval in advance, which in the end may be denied. In either event this can take several months.

In the unlikely event that the only way the merger can be accomplished is through the dissolution of both corporations and the formation of a new, third, organization, you will have a long wait as you incorporate a new nonprofit entity (a simple procedure) and then secure a new 501(c)(3) designation from the IRS. This latter step can take from three months to a year and typically involves more substantial legal assistance and thus higher cost.

The legal implementation of a merger can take anywhere from a month to a year from the day of decision

In summary, the legal implementation of a merger can take anywhere from a month to a year from the day of decision. The amount of time required for your specific situation will depend upon how the transaction is structured, as well as how much attention you can devote to shepherding the process along. In any event, you will need to consult a nonprofit attorney at this point in order to confirm the appropriateness of your preferred method of merger and, depending upon which method is selected, to generate the paperwork that will actually cause it to occur.

Legal counsel

In business mergers, lawyers—sometimes legions of them—are kept busy negotiating the deal and trying to gain advantages for their clients. In nonprofit mergers, absent the profit motive, and indeed, absent actual "owners," it is usually best if the partnership is negotiated directly by the parties. The parties are usually represented by their boards and executives, perhaps using a consultant skilled in the area of nonprofit mergers as facilitator. However, once a "deal in principle" has been struck, it is necessary to consult an attorney, who will

- Review your proposed plans for appropriateness
- Ensure compliance with all federal and state laws
- Protect your IRS exemption
- Execute any legal documents required
- Exercise the prudence required in any major undertaking with legal ramifications

One attorney would never represent both parties to a business merger, but this is precisely the way to do it in the nonprofit world. If you plan to negotiate the terms of the merger yourselves, perhaps using a consultant to assist with facilitation, then hiring two attorneys, each billing you separately, would be redundant and an unnecessary expense. Also, if all of the issues between the parties have been resolved directly by the parties themselves through the negotiations process, the legal function is simply to review and then implement the decisions.

In fact, hiring separate attorneys to represent each party would slow the process, complicate it, raise expenses, and potentially create an adversarial relationship that could affect the outcome of the talks. Thus our recommendation is to hire an attorney jointly, and to bring him or her into the picture only after the "deal in principle" has been agreed to.

One attorney would never represent both parties to a business merger, but this is precisely the way to do it in the nonprofit world

The structure of our legal system makes it difficult for attorneys to represent both parties in any transaction. This problem arises from our system's assumption that virtually all legal proceedings involve an adversarial relationship. Since your merger is probably not adversarial, you will need to search a bit to find an attorney willing to represent both parties. Ask other nonprofit leaders whom they have used, or call local foundations who usually have located and retained the best nonprofit lawyers in the area. Normally an attorney can address the ethical issue by asking both parties to sign a "waiver of conflict" acknowledging that they are both represented by the same law firm. Attorneys who regularly work with nonprofits will be more familiar with this concern and more amenable to your request.

Sometimes expert legal advice is needed on a substantive issue raised by the merger. For example, if one party has a collective bargaining agreement, you should consult a labor attorney to clarify your position; if there are potential antitrust issues, such as in the merger of two hospitals, a health care antitrust attorney should be consulted; if your board is concerned about a disputed property line, a real estate attorney could help.

Once you reach an agreement to merge, it is essential to hire an attorney experienced in *nonprofit* mergers. We have worked with attorneys who claim such experience, but who really only have experience with business mergers. Typically, these attorneys minimize the differences between nonprofit and business mergers, causing nonprofit clients to waste time and money while the attorney either recommends the wrong steps or learns on the job. A favorite example from real life is the attorney who recommended that the best way for two nonprofits to merge was for one to issue stock and the other to purchase it. This inappropriate translation of corporate practice created a great deal of confusion for my clients.

Another concern is the tendency to ask an attorney—any attorney—to do the work pro bono. There are two problems with this: an attorney who does not know nonprofit law will be of little help; and pro bono jobs are often low priority, thus taking longer. You would not take your child to a dermatologist friend to set a broken bone, even if the dermatologist agreed to do it "pro bono." Cost is not the only—or even the major—concern here. As we said earlier, you must find an attorney who knows nonprofit law. The transactions required for a nonprofit merger are fairly simple, but if they are carried out incorrectly a variety of ills could ensue. More likely, an attorney who is not experienced in the area will confuse the boards of directors with unclear messages, cause unnecessary delay, and potentially raise concern and conflict over issues that should have been routine and trouble-free.

Our advice then: hire an attorney who is a nonprofit specialist. She or he will understand the issues, advise you appropriately, carry out the implementation quickly, and probably cost you less money in the long run. When selecting the attorney, ask for references of nonprofit clients, and check them out.

Board Integration

As soon as the boards vote to merge, it is important to find opportunities for them to begin working together. This is especially important for those board members who were not on the merger negotiations committee, and most especially for any board members who might have been hesitant about the merger from the outset.

If a joint board retreat has not already taken place as part of the negotiations process (sometimes this is an important step prior to a vote), this would be a good time to hold one. The retreat could involve the launch of a new strategic planning effort for the combined organizations, board training in fundraising or strategic thinking, a presentation on the market conditions facing the merging organizations, or an overview of the programs offered by the soon-to-be-merged entity. The retreat could provide an opportunity to bring in an outside speaker on a topic of mutual interest, or to undertake a board/staff team-building process. There are plenty of topics you might profitably pursue at this point; choose one that gives the newly merged board the opportunity to begin to work together.

Board retreats allow participants to share the camaraderie and the vision for the future that began to develop during the negotiation process

Whatever the agenda of the retreat, allow adequate time for socialization. If the group is large, you might want to assign seating at tables to ensure that members of the two boards mix. (Color coding name tags is an easy way to do this.) Scatter the staff who will be attending the event among the tables as well. The most important goal for this event is to begin to share more broadly both the camaraderie and the vision for the future that have begun to develop among the negotiators.

Board leadership

One way in which nonprofits help to build trust during the negotiations process is to agree that the board officer slots will be equitably distributed during the first two years after the merger. For example, the matrix in Figure 7 is common. ABC and XYZ, upon merging, agreed to rotate board officers in the manner shown.

In this way each merging organization's board is assured that it will share in the leadership of the merged organization. By the end of the second year, attachment to the former organization is usually less than that to the new one, and the board can go about choosing its officers using more traditional methods.

Figure 7. Transitional Board Officer Assignments

	ABC Nonprofit	XYZ Nonprofit
Year 1	President Secretary	Vice President Treasurer
Year 2	Vice President Treasurer	President Secretary

Some board members may complain that this process is overly artificial. They are perhaps embarrassed by its tit-for-tat, almost childlike, sense of fairness. Sometimes boards want to discard the formula, either from the outset or midway through the two-year period, in favor of trusting the new, combined board to choose the best leaders. Other boards are comforted by the enforced fairness of this initial set of decisions, which allows time for trust to grow. In any event, suggesting this formula for the selection of officers will inevitably lead to a discussion of the important issues of trust and leadership in the new organization. Whether the formula is used or not is less important in the end than the opportunity for the board members to openly discuss and agree upon transitional leadership issues.

The new organization's officers, however chosen, should meet with the nominated executive director as soon as possible to discuss matters such as how board meetings should be run, what the agendas should look like, what materials should be sent out in advance of meetings, how the expectation for annual board donations to the organization will be handled, and so forth. This meeting should ideally take place prior to the first post-merger meeting of the board, affording an opportunity for board and staff leaders to "get their act together" in advance of this crucial board meeting. It is important that the first combined meeting of the two former boards be well organized, interesting, upbeat, and filled with content. Prior planning will help it to be a positive experience for all, thus setting the tone for the new board.

Similarly, the membership of the new board should be surveyed to determine each member's individual interest in committee assignments. This can be done either on the telephone or by mail. While it may not be possible to accommodate every preference, this method is far better than simply assigning people to committees based either on their prior committee experience, their profession, or the whim of the new president. A board member may be tired of serving on the personnel committee after three years; another, a CPA, may prefer to get off the finance committee and into development or governance issues. The fact is, you simply won't know what board members want until you ask them.

The membership of the merged board should be viewed in the same way a slate of new board members is viewed in a well-functioning nonprofit: they are a group of enthusiastic people who have been brought on the board in order to contribute, and they must be educated, supported, and directed in ways that allow them to begin making that contribution as soon as possible, lest their enthusiasm wane.

Systems Integration

Nonprofits develop systems for the management of everything from office supplies to donor names. When two nonprofits merge, these systems must also merge. Some more visible items, such as the accounting system, may be subject to debate in the negotiations committee. Most often, and for most systems, these decisions will be viewed as operational and left to the staff to work out. There is no right way to integrate systems. It is essential, however, to identify the areas where integration will occur and to approach each one with openness and respect for the other group.

Exhibit 8, Systems Requiring Integration, below, lists the systems that most commonly need attention during a merger. For each area needing integration a team composed of people from both organizations should be charged with developing

Exhibit 8. Systems

❏ **Accounting System:** all subsystems, hardware, and software

❏ **Budgeting Process:** who is involved, timing of process, format of presentation

❏ **Payroll System:** frequency of payment, direct deposit options, even which checks to use

❏ **Human Resources Management Systems:** performance reviews, personnel policy development and review, pay scales, bonus and incentive programs, employee benefit programs, employee recognition programs

❏ **Information Systems:** general mailing lists, donor data, service utilization data, management reports

❏ **Purchasing Processes:** authorization processes, any group purchasing agreements

❏ **Inventory and Control Systems:** storage, transportation, quality assurance

❏ **Building and Major Equipment Maintenance Schedules:** planned replacement schedules, deferred maintenance issues, relations with major contractors

❏ **Risk Management Policies and Processes:** insurance coverage, self-insurance arrangements, insurance risk pools, workplace safety plans, emergency response plans

❏ **Annual Calendar of Donor Events, Solicitations, and other Fundraising:** major and small donor campaigns, annual dinners, recognition programs, all stewardship activities

❏ **Strategic Planning and Monitoring Processes:** all aspects of strategic and operational planning

❏ **Outcome Measurement Systems:** the development of measures, staff training in their use, and reporting requirements both internally and externally

recommendations. In most cases this will be a wholly staff-driven process with final sign-off provided by the executive director, not the board. (Of course, the board should be kept apprised of the progress on systems integration.)

Management Integration

Once there is a decision to merge, the combined board of the merging entity should choose an executive director to lead the effort. Beyond this, there is no prescribed way for selecting the other members of the management team. In some cases the various positions and their occupants are agreed upon as part of the negotiations process. More frequently, however, the board and executive director work out what positions are necessary, or the board simply dictates how many positions (or how much money) the executive director may allocate for management. The board may also give a general directive to use the existing managers "to the extent they can fill the bill," again leaving the actual decisions to the executive director.

Both common sense and fairness dictate that the current managers at the two organizations should be looked to first to fill slots on the management team of the merged organization. If there is to be a great deal of management consolidation (for example, there are currently two chief financial officers, two development directors, two operations officers, or too many program directors), distribute the remaining positions among the managers of the two organizations in a manner that will be perceived as fair, both internally and externally.

When assembling management teams, the internal and possibly external political ramifications of personnel choices must also be examined

This concern for fairness most emphatically does *not* mean that managers coming from the merging organizations simply divide the jobs equally. That would probably lead to some very poor choices and long-term headaches. The "perception of fairness" issue *does* mean, however, that in addition to all the other factors the executive director must take into account in assembling a management team (skills, character, contacts, diversity, experience, the ability to function as part of a team) the internal and possibly external political ramifications of these choices must also be examined.

Let's assume, since it is the most frequent situation, that the incumbent executive director of one of the merging organizations is selected by the board to lead the post-merger nonprofit. What should this executive director do if, in all honesty, he or she feels that his or her pre-merger organization's top managers are uniformly better qualified than those of the other group? This is a fairly common scenario.

First, before settling too easily on such a conclusion, consider the criteria on which it is based. Evaluating job qualifications is an inherently subjective activity. The people you know, those who work in your organization, and those in the other organization who act, think, and perhaps even look like your people, will naturally have an edge in your mind, consciously or unconsciously. This does not necessarily make them the best choices.

Moreover, the criteria used for hiring decisions, even among enlightened non-profit leaders, almost inevitably tend to be value-biased. These value filters might favor the traditional "hard skills," the more humanistic "soft skills," or other attributes unique to your organizational culture, such as political commitment or religious affiliation. In assembling your team keep in mind that assembling a diverse group can be the secret to creating a more dynamic new management team. Diversity in this context means *differences* along the full range of human characteristics, from gender, ethnic, and lifestyle differences to unique problem-solving, creativity, and work style approaches.

Management team diversity is important (beyond the obvious social benefits) because it provides the group with greater access to new ideas, different perspectives on issues that come before the organization, novel interpretations of organizational culture, and a range of problem-solving options that far exceeds those available to a more homogenous work group. From twenty years as a nonprofit manager I can say with confidence that a management team that is diverse in many ways is almost always more effective in the long run, if it is managed effectively. Forming such a team is not a quick or easy process; it requires a real effort to see the unique value of each person from a perspective that goes beyond self-imposed limitations.

Reward Staff for Advancing Integration

During the first year after the merger the executive director could offer a monthly prize (maybe dinner for two) to the management team member who does the most to foster cross-staff integration.

Management team selections are frequently based only on the narrowly defined skills that are necessary to the merged organization, and a sense that "I could work with him or her." It is important, however, to also consider essential human and political concerns such as easing the cultural tensions created by the merger, enhancing or preserving the diversity of the previous management teams, maintaining a link to the whole board, and the incalculable value of having managers who know the "other" organization.

Management consolidation that results in the wholesale demotion or dismissal of one nonprofit's previous management team or the selection of a team dominated by a single demographic profile can disrupt the new organization, with ripples extending to funders and the community. This is especially likely if there had previously been greater diversity in one of the organizations. It could take years to recover from the internal and external negative reactions to such a move. The wise executive director will recognize that these are not only personnel decisions, they are also political decisions, with political repercussions that must be taken into account.

There are several benefits to assembling a diverse management team that represents the fullness of the pre-merger organizations. When it comes to attacking the multitude of problems management will face in the merger implementation phase:

- Both technical and interpersonal problems will be more easily identified, categorized, and understood.

- There will be less of a tendency to blame either group for unanticipated problems which crop up.

- Viewed across systems and cultures, the true nature of underlying problems will reveal themselves more quickly, saving time and energy.

In assembling the management team it sometimes happens that a demotion is necessary. This usually occurs when a shuffling of responsibilities results in someone being reassigned to a position generally perceived as having less stature and responsibility. (At least it seems that way to the individual in question.) To ease the move, perhaps the old, higher salary can be retained, or perhaps a new title (which costs nothing) can be created, or a previous work space maintained. Any or all of these actions can help to preserve the person's dignity.

Once the decisions on the composition of the management team are made, they should be announced all at once. A single announcement of any job losses, awful as it might be, is better than making a few decisions this week (which will inevitably make someone unhappy), and a few more the next. After the announcement, all who remain can thus be assured that there are no future reductions in workforce planned. Anyone whose position will change, or who will lose his or her job, should be taken care of as well as is possible. Offer severance packages, early retirement, and other inducements to the extent financially possible.

If the merged board wants a smoothly functioning management team and staff, it must create a smoothly functioning board

Once all the decisions are made and announced, the new management team should hold an extended meeting, perhaps off site, so the members can get to know one another. The executive director should set a tone at this meeting that emphasizes the future, unity, and a lack of favoritism. Avoid comments or jokes that require an insider's knowledge from one of the pre-merger organizations. Consciously consider what messages, practices, values, and rituals to establish in the new team, and begin to convey them, both in word and in deed, at once.

One final thought on management integration: Consider the importance of modeling for staff. If the management team wishes to quell unrest among the merged frontline staff and encourage them to work together harmoniously, one of the most significant things it can do to effect this behavior is to model it in the management team itself. The analogy holds with the board as well. If the merged board wants a smoothly functioning management team and staff, it must create a smoothly functioning board. In both cases this modeling will be far more effective than lectures or memos urging "cooperation."

Staff Integration

The number one fear of staff in many mergers is loss of employment. The truth is that the people most likely to lose their jobs in a nonprofit merger are, in order of likelihood: the executive director, members of the bookkeeping and accounting staff, and middle managers. Because most nonprofits are short on frontline staff, few mergers result in job loss among this group.

Frontline program staff will likely have the greatest fears over job loss, for several reasons. First, they are at the bottom of the corporate ladder and may thus feel powerless and expect bad things to be done to them. Second, they are usually not well informed about the motives for the merger or the details of its execution, a situation that can lead to wild rumors. Third, they hear about business mergers in which wholesale layoffs occur, and may assume that this will also be their fate.

Often, the merger occurred in part because one of the nonprofits was facing a financial crisis. The job losses resulting from this crisis might be decided upon and announced through or during the merger process. In reality such losses would have occurred with or without the merger, and in fact, they might have been worse if not for the merger. Nonetheless, the proximity in time between the merger and job losses, the general stress level in the organization, and the natural desire to find a cause for one's misery will lead many staff to blame the merger, and the merger partner, for the outcome.

Communication is key in any merger, but especially so in the situation just described. Organizational leaders must strive to keep everyone informed of all decisions and their reasons. As with management consolidation, any and all job losses should be announced at the same time, so that a statement of reassurance can be given to the remaining staff. Again, severance pay, help with finding other jobs, or the opportunity to fill other, vacant positions within the organization will help staff and the larger community to feel that the organization is taking good care of its people.

Staff integration is often the most difficult type of integration to achieve. Typically, turnover in the period after a merger will increase, staff stress levels will rise, and communication will become more difficult. Remember to look at it from the perspective of the frontline staff. They will often see very little change in their daily work after the merger, may have little contact with anyone from the newly merged part of the organization, and may have paid little attention during the process. They may be unhappy, unsure of what is going to happen (or even what has happened), and may feel threatened. And day in and day out, they still have their essential jobs to perform.

There are several positive steps management can take to help ease the integration process:

- Form cross-functional teams to develop and propose solutions to the systems integration issues enumerated earlier.

- Combine the training and staff development functions of the two former organizations, and those of any departments doing training on their own, under a committee composed of frontline and management representatives from both former staffs. Use the greater size of the organization to provide a higher level of training at the agency level than was possible for either group before, and don't be shy about pointing out this fact.

- Organize site visits and work teams among staff with analogous roles. Such meetings have three functions: they help people get to know one another; they begin the integration of systems, processes, and standards; and they help to create better inter-program referrals of clients. For example, after merging, two domestic violence organizations set up meetings between their respective staffs: between shelter workers, between outreach workers, and between crisis line workers. This effort helped the staff get started on integration plans and countered some prior negative experiences.

- Address any complaints or troublesome rumors that might emerge about specific programs, people, or functions of the merged organization ("I heard their daycare center spanks kids who misbehave"). Designate staff liaisons to hear the complaint, investigate it, and report their findings. Such liaisons must have great integrity, tact, and obvious impartiality. They should be appointed by the executive director and report their findings to the management team as well as to whomever initiated the complaint. Liaisons should be selected from frontline staff of *both* former organizations.

The bottom line is that staff integration takes time, attention and great patience. It is ultimately the responsibility of the executive director, who will not be able to accomplish much in this area without the support of the management team. Loss of productivity, increased turnover, employee grievances, and even lawsuits can emerge from staffs that do not cohere.

Staff integration takes time, attention and great patience. It is over only when the staff truly feels unified.

The entire integration process can take from six months to three years. It is over only when the staff truly feels unified. When this point is reached is a subjective judgment at best, and it will probably take longer than you expect. We know of a situation where one of the pre-merger organizations' staff experienced 100 percent turnover during the first two years after the merger, and this *still* did not result in a resolution of the integration issues. Somehow, the negative stereotypes about the "other" and the sense of victimization that these staff carried came to be part of the culture of their program, surviving long after they were all gone. As the executive director put it

> *There must be something in the water at that building. People who are new immediately start complaining about things they know nothing about—incidents that happened (or were imagined to have happened) years ago to a group of employees who are no longer with us. I was there and they weren't, but their take on what happened is unshakable.*

Staff integration is more difficult in organizations that are large or have dispersed sites. Distance makes regular contact among the separate programs and between the programs and central management difficult. It also engenders the development of subcultures at isolated sites. One nonprofit organization I ran opened an office in a suburb thirty miles away. We came to refer to this site as "Fort Apache," meaning it was on the frontier, remote from the home office in every way. For ten years this site was an orphan within our growing organization, until a program director was hired who made it her priority to bring the program in line with the larger agency. Not surprisingly, when I left the organization some years later this program director was hired to succeed me as executive director.

Staff integration can be enhanced by cross-organization assignments, teams that involve people from both pre-merger organizations, and all the other suggestions made previously. Unfortunately, none of these is a panacea. The process simply takes time. It is a vitally important process, however, as an organization's greatest resource is its people. It is not just a cliché that a house divided against itself cannot stand; it is a very real truth in a nonprofit merger. Thus staff integration may pose one of the most difficult challenges management will face after merging. It is at the same time one of the most significant and crucial hurdles to success. It can become a true test of leadership.

Managing Culture Conflict

Every merger brings together two cultures, two sets of world experience. The key to successfully integrating these cultures is to recognize them as two distinct ways of seeing and of being which need to first be made explicit, and ultimately brought into harmony.

Anticipate that a few months into merger implementation, some conflict will arise. It may be between the development office and the accounting office (as in the example below) or between two programs. Often, the conflict will be ascribed to someone lacking competence, friendliness, or follow-through. Upon closer examination, however, it may be that the conflict arises out of cultural differences.

The development director from the former ABC nonprofit was accustomed to getting monthly reports from the accounting department that she could reconcile with her donor records. The chief financial officer, who was from the former XYZ nonprofit, had never been asked to provide these reports in the past and thought the request conveyed a lack of trust. Feelings hardened and tempers shortened.

The conflict was resolved when each party explained his or her position. The development director, whose previous, smaller nonprofit, had an unsophisticated finance office, felt it was her responsibility to "check things out" each month and make sure donations were being credited to the proper accounts. The chief financial officer, who prided himself on tracking a multitude of funding sources, felt insulted. With a facilitator, they reviewed together the process for ensuring donations were properly accounted for. At the end of this meeting the development director expressed relief. "I never liked having to review these accounting decisions, and now I feel I don't have to."

Manage the Work of Implementation

To effectively manage their most precious resource—time—executive directors can make a short list (no more than four items) of the most significant issues they must address in the coming week. The items on the list should not necessarily be the most pressing issues— those that everyone is screaming about. Instead, the items should have strategic value to the merged organization, and should require the *personal* efforts of the executive director. Everything else should be delegated.

Once in the office, the executive director will be deluged with important issues and distracted by a steady tide of trivia, minutia, and bureaucratic effluvia. Although it is impossible to ignore these distractions completely, periodic review of the list will remind the executive of the truly important issues. Among these in the first year after a merger is staff integration.

The chief financial officer expressed admiration for his colleague's concern for proper accounting. "It wouldn't be a bad thing if we had more people around here who took that level of interest in getting things straight."

Conflicts such as this are typical in newly merged nonprofits. They become a problem only when the source of the issue gets personalized, as can happen easily in the charged environment of a newly merged organization. Their real source is often a different way of doing things, or of seeing the world. The development director in the example above knew of only one kind of finance department—one that could not be trusted to give accurate information. Although the merger with a larger nonprofit might have suggested to her that this would change, she simply assumed that the adaptations she had made to the situation in her old organization were universally required. She probably never consciously thought about it.

Leaders must seed a new culture, tend it, and help it to take root

The chief financial officer, for his part, assumed that his work would be accepted at face value by everyone in the new organization for no other reason than that it had always been taken as gospel in his old organization. He was unaware of the different experiences of people coming from the other organization and of the different expectations those experiences would create.

To avoid the escalation of situations like this, managers must make a point of tracing conflicts, disagreements, or disparaging remarks to their source. As a good manager in a merged nonprofit, you must sometimes play the role of detective to find the source of the initial misunderstanding. Of course there are still personality conflicts, incompetent employees, and other *real* problems. The task is to sort these difficulties into one category and the misunderstandings, strained relations, and hard feelings caused by the cultural differences that come to light in a merger into another.

Meanwhile, an effort must be made to create a new culture. Corporate culture is composed of unspoken understandings, normative (but unwritten) practices and traditions, and stories involving cultural heroes. As soon as possible after effecting the merger, begin to consciously create new traditions and tell new stories. The merger experience itself provides plenty of raw material. Resist the urge to view corporate culture as a natural phenomenon beyond the reach of conscious influence ("We just have to let a new culture develop in its own sweet time"). The strength of the old cultures will make this difficult. Leaders must seed a new culture, tend it, and help it to take root. Worksheet 21, Integrating Cultures, on page 223, will help you think about how to create a new culture. A sample follows.

WORKSHEET 21 °Integrating Cultures

Develop three new traditions that will be unique to the merged nonprofit. A tradition is anything that involves a large number of employees, is fun, and can be repeated. It could be an annual holiday party, a staff appreciation day, a softball team, or something as simple as having food at all staff meetings. Resist the urge to import traditions from the old organizations. Develop some traditions that are completely new, or at least adapted with a significant new twist.

New Traditions:

1. **Every Friday at 3:00 p.m. we will have a coffee and cookie break in the big conference room.**

2. **Each of our organizations always had small, lunch time holiday parties in the past. As a new organization we will expand this, and have a celebration dinner with a band each year.**

3. **We will put fresh flowers in each department on Monday mornings.**

Develop two stories about the new organization. Tell them at staff meetings, and encourage their spread to new employees as they are hired. An appropriate story could be a funny incident that occurred during the merger negotiations, a misunderstanding caused by the cultural differences of the organizations (and then cleared up), or a battle fought (and won) with a funder who was reluctant to transfer a contract from one group to the other. The stories should express an insider's perspective, pride in the nonprofit, a sense of the organization's uniqueness, a commitment to excellence, or esprit de corps.

New Stories:

1. **People from one of our organizations always dressed very formally for meetings, while people from the other dressed very casually. At the first merger negotiations meeting each group decided to dress like the other group typically did in order to show respect. Everyone looked out of place!**

2. **We held a raffle at our merger celebration party, and one of the prizes was won by a woman whom no one recognized. When she went up to accept, she noticed the T-shirt worn by the emcee with the name of our new organization on it. She asked (close to the microphone!) what that shirt was for and then said, "You mean this isn't the Rotary Party?"**

Creating an Implementation Plan

As you can see, the tasks, issues, and challenges involved in implementation and integration are complex. We advise our clients to begin the process by making an implementation plan. The initial version of this document does not need to be all-inclusive, or even highly detailed. Its purpose is to serve as a guide for the organizations involved, outlining the major considerations and setting a time frame for action with regard to both implementation and integration. A first draft can be prepared by the executive directors of the merging organizations, volunteers from the merging organizations' boards, the nominated executive director of the merged organization, or an implementation steering committee. More detail can be added to the plan as implementation and integration efforts move forward.

A sample implementation/integration plan is included in Appendix E on page 167.

Focus on Mission during Implementation and Integration

Sometimes during implementation and integration, old disputes arise again or new difficulties threaten to derail the process. While the origins of these issues will vary tremendously, we have found it helpful to bring the parties together, review the merger agreement, and highlight the mission-advancing reasons why they agreed to merge in the first place. This is not a "reopening of negotiations," but rather a reminder of what has already been agreed to and why.

Chapter Summary

Implementation of a merger agreement is in some ways straightforward: You file the appropriate papers and wait the necessary time, and you are merged. Integration of people and processes is a more complex process, however, and will take far longer than the legal paperwork.

As a first step, a nonprofit specialist lawyer should review and approve any agreement reached by the boards. He or she will be able to advise the organizations on the most appropriate legal procedure to use. It is also important to begin board integration as soon as the boards vote to merge, and to clarify the leadership of the new board.

Systems integration can involve many things: accounting systems, budgeting processes, human resource management, management information systems, building and equipment maintenance schedules, development systems and procedures, strategic planning and monitoring processes, and many other systems. Specialists may be needed to assist with one or more of these areas.

Integration of management and staff is a crucial part of the implementation process, as is handling the departure or demotion of any employees in an open, respectful manner. Along similar lines, attention must be paid to managing the blending of organizational cultures, and dealing with any culture clash issues that arise. With this, as with *all* stages of the process, open communication is a top priority.

The tasks, issues, and challenges involved in integrating organizations are complex. It is wise to begin the process by making an implementation plan, which outlines the major considerations and sets a time frame for action with regard to both implementation and integration.

Case Studies

Stop HIV and Contra SIDA

The Contra SIDA and Stop HIV boards, led by their respective chairs and the merger negotiations committee, drafted an outline of what they expected to take place throughout implementation. The outline included joint board activities, legal obligations, staff integration activities, discussions regarding real estate and choice of sites, and an initial list of media activities.

During negotiations, the two executive directors, in consultation with their accountants and auditors, had put together preliminary projections for budget consolidation. In those projections they were able to keep all current staff and management positions. Thus the life of the recently formed hiring committee was short-lived; in the end the only position to fill was that of executive director. At the committee's first and only meeting, Mary confirmed that she had decided to retire. She asked that her last day of work be the day before the merger became legal, and reiterated her support for Carmen, the current executive director of Contra SIDA, as a candidate for executive director. The committee reviewed the current budget and recommended the following: to accept Mary's letter of resignation; to offer Mary a six-month severance package; to offer Carmen the position of executive director of the merged entity, at a salary equal to Mary's current salary (higher than Carmen's at Contra SIDA); and to ask the departing executive director to work closely with the incoming executive director to accomplish any necessary tasks before the merger legally took effect. This final recommendation was presented as a condition of Mary's severance package.

In March, the boards held a joint meeting to receive the recommendations of the hiring committee. All recommendations were adopted. After carefully studying the pros and cons, the two boards voted to "interlock" in the period before the merger became legal, in order to create a single board that could communicate better and act more expeditiously.

The newly interlocked boards decided to hold a joint retreat to work on vision and mission and enjoy social activities. They went to a farm-turned-retreat-center in the country. The retreat was a success; integrated mission and vision statements for the new entity were drafted and adopted, and they celebrated the merger. Social activities included a wine and cheese reception, a dance party, and a volleyball game.

The staffs also organized an off-site joint retreat, and several board members attended that event as well. Similar visioning and recreational activities took place. The two staffs celebrated joining forces with their colleagues in the fight against HIV/AIDS.

In a nutshell...

Stop HIV and Contra SIDA

The boards concentrated their efforts on implementation; the executive directors on budget consolidation. The boards also decided to "interlock" for a brief period and attended a joint retreat. They hired an attorney to execute all legal documents and appointed an integration committee to spearhead the work of the merged entity. A merger celebration was organized. New rituals and traditions were suggested and became part of the implementation process.

Seeing the merger as a great fundraising opportunity, the two executive directors worked together to organize a high-profile celebration. Media outlets were targeted, and city officials, large donors, foundation representatives, agency staff, board members, and clients were all invited. The celebration was a success: the Sunday paper and the 10 P.M. News covered it, and several large donations were received at the event. A contest was also held to choose a name for the merged organization. Ballots had been sent out and collected prior to the event, and the winner was announced at the end of the day. The winning entry and new name for the organization was "Counter HIV."

The interlocked boards hired a nonprofit lawyer to review and execute all legal documents related to the merger. They asked the lawyer to comment on their desire to execute a merger in which Stop HIV would dissolve into Contra SIDA, explaining that they wanted to maintain Contra SIDA's special federal grantee status. They also explained that Stop HIV was slated to receive a bequest from a wealthy, terminally ill donor in the near future. After reviewing all pertinent documents, the lawyer advised the group to go forward with their current plan. "All of your projections and plans seem to be within the law, and you should not have any problems maintaining your federal status and claiming your bequest when it is made," he said. The attorney suggested informing the donor of Stop HIV's plans to merge, which was done. The only other comment the lawyer made was that they did not have to give up Stop HIV's tax exempt status right away. He described how they could legally wait until their bequest came through, and then file for dissolution—thus avoiding any potential for difficulty. The board discussed this and decided to follow the lawyer's advice.

At their April meetings, the interlocking boards appointed an integration committee. This committee was made up of individuals associated with both agencies who either had experience with operational integration issues, or who worked in related fields and could help. The integration committee was made up of the following people:

- The two executive directors
- Contra SIDA's board treasurer
- Two accountants and one auditor (on a limited-time basis)
- A board member who was a systems analyst
- One development staff member from each organization
- Two information system staff members from Stop HIV
- A relative of a staff member who was a computer networks specialist
- A pro bono consultant from a local management service organization who had participated in several systems integration projects for nonprofits

The primary goal for staff integration was to retain all current line staff from both agencies to the extent that it was feasible and prudent. The integration committee recommended the formation of cross-functional teams at all levels of the new organization to come up with suggestions on integration issues. They held an all-day session with these teams, giving everyone an opportunity to contribute to the process by brainstorming and drawing schematics of how they thought their systems could be best integrated. The integration committee was pleased with the input, as these were the very people who would be using the integrated systems.

Two meetings later, the integration committee brought its recommendations to the full board. The quality of the suggestions and the accuracy of their descriptions was applauded. Carmen presented a detailed implementation plan that spanned eighteen months, after which it was projected that full systems integration would be accomplished. The newly interlocked boards reviewed the plan and cast a unanimous vote of approval for it.

Culture conflict was not visible during the first few months of the merger process. Whenever it was time to practice an accustomed ritual from one of the former agencies, the group spearheading the effort would invite staff members from the other pre-merger organization to join. Eventually, it became common practice to try to maintain all the rituals that both agencies brought with them.

Carmen asked staff to suggest new traditions for the merged organization, promising to try as many as possible, and to time-test those suggested to see which ones became most popular. The staff came back with a number of great suggestions; the cultural calendar quickly filled with exciting new traditions. A year into the integration process, Counter HIV had integrated the following traditions into their organizational lives: an annual picnic with sports and outdoor activities; monthly staff meetings; birthday celebrations; a benediction of the new year by the executive director in January; potlucks when anyone left the agency; and a Christmas party for clients and their families.

Community Arts Center and Museum of Art and Culture

Once the boards of Community Arts Center and Museum of Art and Culture voted to merge, they each nominated two board members to work with the executive directors and key management staff to plan the implementation of the merger. They also discussed how they would communicate the news to their staff, donors, and patrons. They decided to send individual letters to their donors, to put an article in their respective newsletters to notify their patrons, and to call immediate all-staff meetings to announce the decision within their own organizations. They left plans for other public announcements, celebrations, and so forth up to the implementation committee.

In a nutshell...

Community Arts Center and Museum of Art and Culture

An implementation committee was organized to make a public announcement of the merger, retain a lawyer to finalize the merger, plan a retreat, and begin to plan the process of implementation. Staff integration was challenging; job losses occurred and many of the remaining employees struggled with the changes they faced.

The next day the executive directors got together with their development directors to draft a letter to their key donors announcing the decision. After agreeing on the content of the letters, which would be similar, they directed their development directors to print and send them. They also each called an all-staff meeting within their organizations. The meetings had a celebratory air, as well as serving as a forum for questions and an opportunity for people to volunteer to help with the integration efforts. The executive directors explained that full integration would take over a year, but that the goal was to make everyone feel like part of the same organization as soon as possible. "Together we will be stronger, better able to offer a variety of artistic opportunities to the community, and better able to attract the funds we need to grow in the ways that we want," they each told their staffs. They also explained how the new board would be structured: ten of Museum of Art and Culture's fifteen board members would join ten of Community Arts Center's fourteen board members to make a new board of twenty members. While this board would not become official for several months (when the merger became final), they assured everyone that all twenty individuals were working together with the departing board members to oversee the transition process.

The first formal task of the new implementation committee was to retain a lawyer to review the board's agreement and file the necessary papers. The lawyer found no problems with the agreement, and concurred with the boards' assessment that because of Museum of Art and Culture's large endowment, it would be best for Museum of Art and Culture to be the surviving corporation. He also recommended that instead of Community Arts Center *dissolving into* Museum of Art and Culture, it should probably just dissolve and leave its assets to Museum of Art and Culture. "The end result is the same," he informed them, "but since Community Arts Center did get threatened with a lawsuit once, you might want to play it safe and not leave an opportunity for the suit to be reopened with a claim against the new organization." Both boards agreed, and directed the lawyer to file the necessary papers.

In the meantime, the implementation committee attacked its next big challenge: systems integration. The committee gathered the names of the accountants, management information systems staff, human resource managers, operations directors, and development directors from each organization (though in some cases one person fulfilled several of these functions), and asked them to serve on specific integration task forces. Each task force was asked to review how both organizations handled a particular aspect of their operations, and then to recommend how those systems could best be integrated.

The merger negotiations committee had recognized that it might be necessary to let certain administrative staff people go after a merger, and the human resources task force soon confirmed this. It recommended to the executive directors that they offer severance to one of the staff accountants, one membership coordinator, and two of Museum of Art and Culture's part-time art instructors, and allow Ron, as incoming executive director, to manage the process of deciding who should stay and who should be asked to leave. The situation was handled carefully; two employees were referred to other jobs at museums and a third took some time off to be with her family.

A month after the boards agreed to merge they held a joint board retreat. There they took time to learn more about each other's programs, to get to know one another, and to start developing the new vision and strategic direction for the merged organization. The twenty members of the new board pledged to make a strategic planning effort their first focus, and to expand their fundraising efforts in conjunction with a public relations campaign announcing and celebrating the official completion of the merger process.

At the end of the daylong session, staff from both Community Arts Center and Museum of Art and Culture arrived, and together everyone enjoyed a lively barbecue. They finished off the night by telling favorite stories, traditions, and memories about each organization and sharing their passion for art. The name for the new organization was also announced: The Museum of Art and Community Culture. Everyone recognized that while the event was only a beginning, it was a very successful beginning.

Over the next few months Marie Simeon began phasing out of her executive director role and taking on more responsibility for the educational programs at both Museum of Art and Culture and Community Arts Center. Ron Kyle, on the other hand, spent part of his time over at the Community Arts Center facility, learning their operations and preparing to take over as the new executive director. Both took time to adjust to their new roles, and Marie especially had a hard time letting go of some of the decision making that felt so natural to her. She and Ron met often to discuss her feelings, and the two worked together to incorporate her ideas while still keeping her primary focus on developing the educational component of the Museum's mission.

True staff integration was perhaps the biggest challenge. The artistic interests of employees at each of the pre-merger organizations were different, and thus the types of exhibits they managed, classes they taught, and work they did reflected their different aesthetic values. Still, Ron and Marie made sure to put people from the two organizations together on projects as much as possible, and organized regular social events for the entire staff.

Integration was by no means an easy process, but it went fairly well. Two years after the merger, one-third of the staff was new, and The Museum of Art and Community Culture was the pride of the city. The rest of the staff—former employees of Museum of Art and Culture and Community Arts Center—adjusted to the change, and thanks to the continual efforts of Ron and the new board, their allegiances gradually shifted to the new organization. Attendance at all exhibits was up, the roster of classes offered had expanded, and the Museum had formed a new and exciting partnership with local schools that helped introduce area children to a broad range of artistic experiences. "Am I glad we did this?" asked Alexandra Ryan, the new board president. "That's a resounding yes. We've made art more visible, and more available to the community. And that is what we *all* wanted."

CHAPTER 7

Funding a Merger

What is it going to cost? Where will I find the money?

MERGERS entail a variety of front-end costs, most of which are nonre-curring and can be anticipated. The actual costs vary according to the type of partnership involved, the level of changes foreseen, and the availability of in-kind, pro bono or reduced cost alternatives. Lack of funding causes some organizations to avoid some optional costs altogether. In this chapter, you will learn some steps for anticipating the costs of the merger and seeking funds to finance it.

Estimating the Cost

Typical costs to consider include the professional costs of legal counsel and consultants, as well as costs associated with design, printing, signage, severance, moving, and systems integration.

Professional costs

Different professionals may be useful in the development, facilitation, and implementation of your partnership. Frequently consulted professionals include lawyers and consultants.

Lawyers. Depending upon your project, you may require the services of a non-profit lawyer or other specialist to create, dissolve, merge, or alter the structure of one or more nonprofit corporations. Extensive information was given on choosing expert legal counsel in Chapter 6, pages 113–115. Here is a recap of some of the issues:

- If your partnership potentially raises restraint-of-trade issues, consult an antitrust attorney at the outset.

- If the employees of one or more of the potential partners in the merger are unionized, consult a labor attorney.

- If either partner is involved in litigation, a business litigation attorney may help the other party to understand its potential exposure, if any.

- Less frequently, experts in real estate, estate planning, and other specialties may be consulted.

- For the merger itself, seek an attorney with expertise in nonprofit law.

- Avoid the tendency to seek pro bono assistance from an attorney with corporate merger experience; the corporate model does not apply to nonprofit mergers.

To reduce the costs of attorneys in your project use management consultants to facilitate the crafting of your agreements, and then bring in legal counsel at the point where the partners know what they want to accomplish. At this point an attorney can more quickly review your plans and advise you on the best way to achieve your goals. Second, whenever possible, engage joint counsel. This means that all parties to the partnership work together to hire one attorney who works collaboratively with them.

To reduce the costs of attorneys, use management consultants to facilitate the crafting of your agreements, and then bring in legal counsel at the point where the partners know what they want to accomplish

Legal fees vary widely. Nonprofit specialists may be reluctant to discount their fees or to do pro bono work, since most of their clients would ask for a break. Legal fees for a simple merger can range from $5,000 to $7,500 and up. More complex partnerships or contentious mergers can dramatically increase fees.

Consultants. Most mergers will benefit from the services of a competent non-profit management consultant. While there is no uniform licensing or certification for consultants, they do tend to develop specialties such as fundraising, strategic planning, board development, finance, or human resource issues. Finding a consultant who specializes in nonprofit mergers can be difficult, but locating one with prior experience in the area is essential.

A consultant can help the parties to determine their goals; can organize, facilitate, and shepherd the process through to completion; and can anticipate and help to resolve roadblocks that emerge along the way. Often, a stalled process is revitalized and brought to completion only after a consultant is brought in.

Because a merger is a high-stakes undertaking, it is important to have an outside, neutral facilitator who can guide you through the predictable stages and stumbling blocks.

In addition to a merger specialist, specialized consultants are often needed to integrate personnel systems, financial management and accounting packages, web sites, information systems, or other specialty areas. One way to minimize your troubles is to contract with your merger consultant to act as a sort of "general contractor" who then recruits and supervises the work of any specialists that are needed. These specialists may be readily available in-house at some consulting firms.

Hourly billing rates for nonprofit management consultants vary widely, depending on region, experience, supply and demand, and other factors; rates range from $40 an hour to more than $200 an hour. In contracting with a consultant, ask for a work plan and a bid for the entire project. For example, you could ask *"What will it take to get us to a decision point? And then what would you do and how much more would you charge to help us to implement it?"* A consultant experienced in mergers should be able to give you a two-phase bid. Phase 1 covers research, facilitation, and decision making. Phase 2 follows up for a specified period as the organizations implement their decision. The work of any subconsultants should also be anticipated and contracted for, either at the outset, or when the need becomes clear. A good resource to help understand what a consultant can and cannot do, and how to structure the contract, is *Succeeding with Consultants,* by Barbara Kibbe and Fred Setterberg (see Resource List).

Design, printing, and signage costs

If your merger involves the creation of a new entity, new name, new program, or a change of address, chances are you will have to update materials such as signs, letterhead, envelopes, brochures, business cards, and other essentials. If a new logo is required, a designer must create one, and it must then be used on new stationery and signs. These costs vary widely, but can be significant. Internal publications staff can lead the way in identifying the necessary specialists and projecting costs.

Severance costs

When employees' positions are eliminated in a merger, it is important to be fair to them, both for the benefit of the employees and for the reputation of the new organization. The manner in which terminated individuals are treated sends a message to the larger community of employees, trustees, donors, and clients about the values of the new organization. The handling of these matters sets a tone (for good or ill) for the overall merger implementation.

We recommend that employees in good standing who have been with the organization at least a year receive a four-to-six month severance package, including pay and health benefits. Outplacement counseling or referrals to new positions can also be helpful. Many nonprofits have severance provisions in their personnel policies. These should be reviewed and followed, both in letter and in spirit.

Moving costs

Sometimes a merger entails moving offices. This may be limited to reshuffling office space within a single building, or might require the movement of people and things from one city to another. In any event, these costs should be anticipated and budgeted.

Systems integration costs

Nonprofit organizations naturally develop a variety of systems for getting things done, ranging from off-the-shelf software solutions for common administrative functions to customized software and idiosyncratic manual and paper-based ways of doing things. Your merger may require the integration of financial and accounting systems and software, web sites, information systems, personnel policies, and compensation plans and systems. Sometimes entirely new systems must be developed to address needs that arise through the merger process. Consultant costs, hardware and software purchases or upgrades, and specialized training are examples of the kinds of costs that should be anticipated here.

One of the costs of your partnership is time: the attention and effort of organizational leaders and staff

Other costs

The partnership you bring about creates many opportunities, and these may in turn require funding to realize. For example, if your merger will attract the attention of civic leaders, philanthropic funders, or potential community donors, it might be wise to invest in public announcements and celebration activities. These activities could require hiring a publicist, creating marketing materials, and the actual costs of any celebrations.

Other potential opportunities include the development of new joint programs with your partner, the purchase of a building, or expansion into new geographic areas. All of these activities will entail costs. Finally, one of the costs of your partnership is *time*: the attention and effort of organizational leaders and staff. Be aware of what you are choosing *not* to do as a result of choosing to engage in a merger.

Worksheet 22, Calculating the Costs of your Merger, page 225, will help you anticipate the costs of your merger. A sample worksheet follows.

WORKSHEET 22   Calculating the Costs of Your Merger

Legal	Nonprofit Attorney	**$5,000**
	Optional Specialists: Labor specialist	
	Business litigation specialist	
	Real estate specialist	
	Antitrust specialist	
Consultants	Merger Consultant/Facilitator	**$15,000**
	Optional Specialists: MIS specialist	**$3,100**
	Finance specialist	**$4,000**
	Human Resource specialist	**pro bono**
Design and Printing	Logo Design	**pro bono**
	Printing	**$8,230**
	Signage	**$3,975**

Severance
1. Weekly Salary **$1000** x **26** weeks + fringe **$5,200** – **$51,000**
2. Weekly Salary_____ x ____weeks + fringe _____ = **(departing**
3. Weekly Salary_____ x ____weeks + fringe _____ = **executive)**
4. Weekly Salary_____ x ____weeks + fringe _____ = _____
   Outplacement Counseling **$1,000**

Moving	Professional Movers	**$1,800**
	Moving allowance for staff	
	Utility/phone hookup	**$500**
Systems Integration	Consultants	
	Hardware (new PC's)	**$4,500**
	Software	**$600**
	Training	
Other Costs	Celebration	**$4,000**
	New space (fix-up)	**$10,000**
	New programs	
TOTAL PROJECTED COSTS		**$92,905**

Strategies for Securing Funding

You should produce an implementation budget as early as is feasible. Once the scope of required funding is known, you can begin identifying and pursuing possible sources.

Foundation grants

A growing number of foundations are willing to support nonprofit mergers. Foundations that fund your programs could be asked for technical assistance grants. Community foundations interested in improving local nonprofit management may also be able to help. As in any grant proposal, the project's goals, time line, justification, and benefits must be clearly articulated. One advantage of such proposals (from the foundations' view) is that the costs are nonrecurring.

Corporate support

Like foundations, many large corporations and local businesses support community agencies. Sometimes a business you approach may itself be the product of a merger or restructuring effort, and hence may have some sympathy for you. The key to most corporate grants is usually personal contacts within the company. Ask your board members, volunteers, and supporters who they know and where they work.

Pro bono contributions

The perils of pro bono legal services were described earlier. However, a graphic artist, printer, software supplier or other vendor may be willing to donate some items, particularly if you have been, and will likely be in the future, a paying customer. Don't be afraid to ask.

Agency reserves

A merger is an unusual occurrence at most nonprofits. Therefore using agency reserves or income from investments for one-time costs may be appropriate. Think it through carefully, however, as reserve spending, once begun, has become a slippery slope for many nonprofits.

Loans

Regional associations of grantmakers (RAGs) may offer loans for nonprofits in specific situations. Ask if your local RAG has such a program and if you qualify. Some foundations also offer loans, called program related investments (PRI). These are usually described in their grant guidelines.

Cost savings

Often we hope a merger will save money. Where there were previously two executive directors, there is now one—or so the thinking goes. Sometimes real savings do occur early after a merger. More likely, severance, the creation of new positions to manage a more complex organization, and the constant demand for more services by clients and communities will devour any projected savings. If possible, budget any short-term savings to cover the one-time costs of the project. Then, when the savings go away, the costs will also be gone.

Chapter Summary

Mergers cost money, and preparation of a thorough, well-thought-out budget is a vital part of a successful merger effort. Relevant costs include professional fees, legal fees, design and production costs, severance costs, moving costs, systems integration costs, and the cost of celebrations and public relations. Possible sources of funding include foundations, corporations, pro bono contributions, agency reserves, loans, and the cost savings that may result from the (typically administrative) efficiencies created by the merger.

Case Studies

Stop HIV and Contra SIDA

Carmen and Mary started working on an implementation budget as soon as a resolution to merge was adopted by the two boards. With the help of their finance staffs, they put together a budget that included both one-time savings and expenses and recurring savings and expenses. This budget underwent seven revisions in a period of two months, and the summarized version looked like this in the end:

One-time costs:

Nonprofit attorney	$4,000
Design of new logo	$2,000
Printing of new brochures, signage, etc.	$13,500
Severance	$31,200
Systems Integration (MIS)	$4,800
Moving	$2,275
Celebration	$5,000
One-time savings (from vacant positions):	(-$10,000)
Total one-time costs:	**$ 52,775**

Recurring savings:

Audit	$5,000
Insurance	$3,000
Salaries	$52,000
Recurring costs (new contract with PR firm):	(-$12,000)
Total recurring savings:	**$ 48,000**

Together Contra SIDA and Stop HIV requested support from their funders, as well as from two corporations with which they were connected through staff and board members. One foundation that had historically funded both agencies granted them $12,000 for technical assistance, and one of the corporations contributed $6,000 for one-time expenses. The remaining funds had to be absorbed by agency reserves. Carmen and Mary decided to share these costs equally.

Community Arts Center and Museum of Art and Culture

Early in the exploration process Community Arts Center and Museum of Art and Culture had applied for and received a joint grant to cover the cost of the nonprofit management consultant (Sara Tyler) that led them through the negotiation process. On her advice, they had also developed a budget for legal services, should a merger be approved and a lawyer be needed. Thus the negotiations committee worked through its issues secure in the knowledge that they could afford *that* process, but knowing that a positive recommendation on their part would result in considerably expanded financial need.

After the boards voted to move forward with a merger, the implementation committee was given the task of drafting an implementation budget. This draft was presented to each board soon thereafter, and the executive directors were charged with working with the development directors to flesh it out and apply for the necessary funds.

Museum of Art and Culture and Community Arts Center were able to identify numerous one-time costs, among them increased salaries for Community Arts Center employees, systems integration costs, design and printing costs for new material, and the costs of public relations and celebrations. They also recognized that if they planned to expand Museum of Art and Culture's facilities to include one or more new wings for Community Arts Center's exhibits, they would need to undertake a capital campaign.

There were also some projected savings, most notably the salaries of the four part-time employees that were being let go. While the administrative and development offices felt they could be more efficient and productive as part of the larger organization, they did not see any substantial cost savings.

After fleshing out their implementation budget and projecting funding and cash flow needs for the merged organization for the next two years, Community Arts Center and Museum of Art and Culture presented joint proposals to several large foundations known to support arts organizations, nonprofit infrastructure, or both. They were fortunate; with the exception of the new space at Museum of Art and Culture's facility, they were given grants to cover over 80 percent of their transitional needs. The new board, encouraged by the news and buoyed by the public relations opportunities available to them, went into high gear to raise money for the new wings. Two and a half years later, the new wings were opened, and the board and development office of the new organization were on to their next challenge.

CHAPTER 8

For Consultants Only

HAVING facilitated more than sixty mergers and other partnerships among nonprofits, I have developed some strong opinions about the role of consultants in these efforts. This chapter will attempt to distill the lessons I have learned and the opinions I have developed into some suggestions for consultants engaged in the difficult work of facilitating mergers among nonprofits. I offer this chapter humbly, realizing how much I still have to learn, and how often I still make mistakes.

The consultant in a nonprofit merger plays a number of roles. Over time it has been necessary for me to assume the following roles, not always willingly:

The Ringmaster—ensuring that each independent act in the circus gets on and off stage at the appropriate time.

The Confessor—confidant to board and executive negotiators and other staff from both parties. People will often reveal amazingly sensitive organizational, personnel, and even personal confidences, for no other apparent reason than that I am perceived as neutral and willing to listen.

The Sage—the hoped-for source of wisdom and advice on everything from nonprofit management to auto repair. (I once left a management team meeting in order to help a staff member who had lost his keys hot-wire his car, a skill retained from my misspent youth.)

The Fortune-Teller—the prognosticator of what the future will bring. Clients have often assumed, unfortunately incorrectly, that I have an uncanny ability to predict everything from future trends in their market to how a given individual will react if his job is eliminated.

The Mediator—the holder of the neutral turf where differences can be resolved.

This is a lot to ask of a consultant, but I think it is all a necessary part of the job. Mergers are the most trying, frightening, disturbing undertakings most nonprofit leaders (both board and staff) will ever experience. These independent, strong-minded individuals often try to make their way through the process on their own, and equally often bog down at some point or other and seek help. When they do, they may be distrustful, concerned, or downright scared.

I have spoken to experienced consultants who have facilitated one merger, or perhaps two, in an entire career of organizational development, strategic planning, marketing, or fundraising consulting. Their consensus is that mergers are related to but inherently different from each of these areas, and require a somewhat different set of skills and a somewhat different attitude on the part of the consultant.

The consultant's challenge in a merger is not just a matter of magnitude; it is primarily a matter of complexity

The most significant way in which mergers differ from other areas of nonprofit management consulting practice is that there are always at least two client organizations. This fact requires a totally different mindset about issues ranging from decision making to communication to confidentiality. Also, the sheer number of people the consultant must interact with is at least double what it is in any other field of practice. Finally, the effort every good consultant makes to understand the culture of the client's organization and to work within that culture is also made more complex by the presence of more than one culture.

We must look beyond the magnitude issue just described for the real challenge. The merger process requires more of the consultant than understanding the culture, people, and communication styles of two or more organizations. This would be difficult enough. However, for the consultant to be effective, he or she must also understand how the different cultures interact, what aspects of each organization's style might set the other organization on a negative course, and what old or new relationships or animosities exist between the organizations and their people. Thus, the consultant's challenge in a merger is not just a matter of magnitude; it is primarily a matter of complexity.

Consider a strategic planning effort, in which the organization's different constituencies—board, clients, line staff, middle managers, senior managers, volunteers, donors, funders (public and private), collaborating agencies, and competitors—are polled, prodded, and vetted so that the organization can learn what it needs to know in order to move forward. Each of these constituencies has a separate, sometimes conflicting, but always valid position on the issues facing the nonprofit.

With two nonprofits you have two sets of such constituencies, and the attempt to reach consensus about what to do can become hopelessly mired in conflicting opinions and needs. Add additional nonprofits (we have worked with as many as nineteen separate parties in one partnership) and the requirements the consultant must meet grow exponentially.

The process recommended in this workbook addresses this complexity by requiring a committee that represents each of the partners in the negotiations. The consultant must continually remind this joint merger negotiation committee of two things:

1) It has a great deal of freedom in designing the merger.

2) It has no authority to implement any plan it develops.

This dialectic allows the process to move forward. The committee, representing its own members' views of the needs of the organizations, can often design a merger that works well. However, the consultant must continually remind the committee of the need to communicate with larger groups—the board and staff and possibly clients or funders—on key points of the agreement they are developing. If this does not occur, the deal might be brilliantly conceived, well-articulated, and ultimately rejected by the respective boards of directors.

The merger consultant represents process. He or she must also represent hope: the hope for success.

The merger consultant, thus, represents process. He or she must also represent hope: the hope for success. At some point in virtually every merger I have facilitated there comes a crisis. Sometimes it arrives early in the process, sometimes near the end. Sometimes there is a series of crises. The stress of the process can bring on the crisis, and sometimes the crisis will spring from the interpersonal stressors of the merger negotiations. It is likely that the crisis will emerge from unspoken feelings or values that finally bubble to the surface. When this happens, disappointment and discouragement may develop among the negotiators.

This situation is akin to the newlywed couple having its first fight and suddenly realizing that their relationship will not necessarily be the bed of roses they hoped for and expected; instead it will be complicated and sometimes even painful. The nonprofit leader, like the newlywed, is likely to experience acute disappointment and distress when faced with an unexpected crisis in the merger negotiation or implementation processes. The role of the merger consultant is to contain the crisis so that the disagreement, hurt, or whatever triggered it, does not generalize to the whole process. It is also his or her role to normalize the experience, to provide a context for the disappointment the negotiators experience, and to help them accept it. Finally, it is the consultant's role to refocus, after working through the crisis, on the hopeful parts of the discussion so that perspective is not lost. In order to do this the consultant must never lose hope himself or herself. Sometimes this calls for all the inner resources the consultant can muster.

In particularly tough situations, I often resort to humor. I find it wonderfully effective at restoring hope, both mine and the clients'. After all, if the consultant, the expert in these matters, is still making jokes, how bad can it be? A couple of my favorite lines:

> *"When you finish this process we'll start a group for adult survivors of merger."*

> *"If we can pull this off we'll all be nominated for the Nobel Peace Prize."*

Hope is a strange, intangible quality, equal parts desire, fantasy, idealism, and pragmatism. Without hope the nonprofit sector would have folded up its tent and gone home a long time ago. The consultant must represent hopefulness, even as he or she embodies helpfulness.

A few specific suggestions for merger consultants:

- As soon as possible after you are initially contacted by someone regarding a new project, suggest a meeting with representatives from both (or all) parties. Even one initial meeting "alone" with the management team or board of "Agency A" could poison "Agency B" toward working with you. Your neutrality must be above suspicion.

- Always contract to represent all parties to the merger, not just one. In a sense, your client is the process itself. Put your contract in writing and have each party sign it.

- Always discuss up front how your fee will be paid and suggest that it be shared among the parties. It need not be split 50/50 by two merger partners if one is larger or wealthier than the other, but both should pay something. The sharing of the fee is essential to each party's sense that it is indeed a *partnership*.

- If one organization tries to get you to align with its position and to help it convince the other "unreasonable" group of the merits of this position, listen respectfully, but stay in the middle, even if you agree with their characterization of the situation.

- If you find yourself talking to one group regularly and avoiding talking to the other group, perhaps because you find its leaders unpleasant, immediately call and reconnect with the leadership of the latter group. You are drifting out of the middle.

- Never reveal any confidence entrusted to you by anyone, at any level, in any of the organizations. If you do reveal such confidences, even once—no matter how well-intentioned—your usefulness to the process will be compromised.

- Be clear on the tasks that merger negotiation participants should accomplish between meetings. (I call this "homework.") Use checklists, memos, or whatever else works for the group. Record these expectations in the minutes. You are a consultant to the process, not just a facilitator of meetings.

- Don't hesitate to tell your clients where you think they may be going wrong. They have hired you not simply as a process facilitator or a scribe to record their discussions, but to offer specific expert advice on their options, and an early warning if they begin to get off course. You must lead them back onto the path. Once there they can make the best decisions for themselves.

- Remember that the role of the consultant is not to produce a merger, but to guide a process that leads to the best result for the organizations involved.

Remember, the role of the consultant is not to produce a merger, but to guide a process that leads to the best result for the organizations involved

Chapter Summary

Consultants play many roles in a merger process: facilitator, advisor, ringmaster, confessor, sage, fortune-teller, and mediator, to name a few. They can be an invaluable asset to the organizations going through the merger, and are a source of stability, process, and hope for all involved. Nonprofit merger consultants must be adept at representing and working with multiple organizations at once, being neutral, communicating clearly and openly, and dealing with the very natural and very common feelings of anxiety and fear that come with such fundamental change efforts.

Appendices

Sample Final Minutes from a Completed Negotiation

Stop Domestic Violence and Salud es Poder Proposed Merger Agreement

Recommendation

The joint merger negotiations committee recommends to the respective boards that they undertake a merger of the organizations, based on the following agreements.

Board issues

The new board will have an authorized maximum of twenty persons. The initial board will be formed of all current board members interested in participating, not to exceed ten from each organization. Any subsequent openings will be filled by agreement of the new board. The new board will have a policy of recruiting 50 percent of its members from north county and 50 percent from south county. It will also maintain at least 50 percent Latino members. Meetings will be scheduled at mutually convenient locations.

There will be the following officers: President, Vice President, Secretary, Treasurer. In the first year post-merger Stop Domestic Violence will appoint the President and Secretary and Salud es Poder will appoint the Vice President and Treasurer. In the second year the President and Vice President will reverse roles. Thereafter, the board will choose its officers freely.

Mission and vision issues

The proposed mission statement for the new organization is: *to end the cycle of violence for all women and children in our communities, with a special commitment to Latinas and other underserved groups.* We meet this mission through shelter, counseling, education, legal, and advocacy services. We value inclusiveness, responsiveness, and an ethic of caring. Our clients come first. The organization must maintain a bilingual, multicultural identity.

Staff and community members will be asked for their ideas on names and a pro bono advertising firm will be asked to help. A decision will be put off until after the decision to merge.

Programmatic issues

No program changes are contemplated as a result of the merger. Several possible growth areas were discussed, including: alcohol and drug counseling, parenting classes, transitional housing, outreach to younger kids experiencing or at risk for relationship violence, legal services, and employability services.

Financial issues

Accounting systems will remain the same. Currently the organizations use the same CPA. For computers, one has PC's and the other has MacIntoshes. For now we will not change this. Stop Domestic Violence's foundation holds some funds for it. Stop's budget is $900,000 and Salud's is $533,000.

The Stop Big City site is leased for about $4,000 per month.
The Stop shelter has a mortgage payment of about $600 per month.
The Salud Small Town site is leased for $1,800 per month.
The Salud shelter is on a lease-option for $1,100 per month.
The Salud Suburb site is on a month-to-month $600 per month rent.

It seems possible to move offices within the next year given many short-term lease arrangements. The boards decided to place the administrative offices in Small Town.

Neither organization revealed anything of substance in the due diligence discussion. There are no legal actions pending or unusual debts. The accountant provided an overview of the organizations' finances. There were no surprises. The new organization will be committed to accumulating three months of operating reserves as soon as is possible. The form of the merger will be determined based on funder requirements.

One organization will be named the surviving corporation, but we will wait until after the next round of funding before actually dissolving the disappearing corporation, in case there is an advantage to having two corporations.

An analysis of increased and decreased expenses for the merged entity will be conducted and submitted to a board in early July. This analysis will include bringing the Salud staff up to the pay and benefit levels of Stop, and will factor in the savings from one executive director position and the combination of audit and insurance activities.

Human resource issues

Stop has a union; Salud does not. The committee obtained legal advice. The committee recommends a neutral stance vis-a-vis a union coming to Salud. It will be up to the employees to decide if they want representation.

Staff presented a side-by-side comparison of jobs and salary ranges. The consultant met with the two executive directors for a preliminary discussion of the senior management positions and their own roles. The executive directors both expressed strong desire for the directorship of the combined agency and no interest in a "number two" position. The committee then determined that there would not be an Associate Executive Director job.

The consultant reported the results of a survey of staff. Two good results to come from the survey and staff meetings include a series of planned meetings between the two staffs, function by function, and the appointment of a liaison person at each agency to receive complaints from the other organization, investigate them, and report back findings. The executive directors have appointed people to these roles.

The committee reviewed staffing in the merged agency, especially in light of staff concerns for job security. The result of this review was as follows:

1. One of the two current executive directors will lose her job in the merger.

2. There are three middle managers in the two organizations, one at Salud and two at Stop. There will probably be three middle management positions in the combined organization, although the final determination of positions will be left to the executive director. Each of the current middle managers will be able to apply for the middle management positions in the new organization. If they qualify for the positions as structured, they will be hired. This determination will be made by the executive director.

3. All other positions (all frontline positions) within the organizations are secure. There will of course be some adjustments in some staff assignments due to the merging of functions. In some cases, people will be able to specialize rather than having to perform parts of several jobs. However, there will be no job losses or cutbacks among frontline staff as a result of the merger.

The executive director selection process will take place after all other issues are resolved. In this way the two directors will not be put through a difficult process and then find out the merger is not going ahead. A committee representing the two boards and a possible outside party will make the selection. Staff will have an opportunity to voice their opinions to the selection committee prior to the decision.

Fundraising and public relations

Funder reaction has been positive. Two public fora were held. A total of seventeen persons who were not from either agency's staff or board attended. The input fell along the following lines: those with general community interest, such as members of the Women's Commission, were positive toward the merger; those with a history of working with Salud feared the loss of the agency's independence, power, and identity, and were therefore opposed to the merger.

The merger will entail some one-time costs for which foundation support will be sought:

Design, printing, and signage	$15,000
Moving expenses	$5,000
Miscellaneous	$5,000
Total estimated one-time merger expense	**$25,000**

Next steps

A special joint board meeting is scheduled for July 15, 6–7:30 PM at the community foundation. Financial information will be reviewed, and a possible vote will be taken on whether to recommend merger to the respective boards.

Pre- and Post-Merger Organizational Profile

THE following instrument is used by La Piana Associates, Inc. to assess the starting point for merger participants. The same instrument is then used again after the merger is implemented in order to determine some of the outcomes of the process. You may find it useful to conduct your own pre- and post-merger surveys to gather outcome information for management, the board, or funders.

Pre- and Post-Merger Organizational Profile

Fill in this sheet for each participating organization at the beginning of a project, and one for any/all resulting organization(s) at the conclusion of the project. We will continue with evaluations at designated intervals thereafter.

Identifying information

Organization name _____

Mission _____

_____

_____

(Considering) partnering with

_____

_____

Subsector ☐ health ☐ human services ☐ environment ☐ arts

☐ advocacy ☐ education ☐ other _____

Geography/Catchment area _____

Date founded _____ **Budget size** _____

Number of staff (FT, PT, and FTE) _____

_____

Primary motivation for strategic restructuring

_____

_____

Source of funds for the strategic restructuring effort

Self	_____ %	(amt: _____)
Local government	_____ %	(amt: _____)
Foundation/Corporate	_____ %	(amt: _____)
Other	_____ %	(amt: _____)
Unfunded need	_____ %	(amt: _____)

Financial indicators

Year			
Total Budget			
Fund Balance amount:			
as a percentage of total assets:			
Current Ratio *current assets ÷ current liabilities*			
Quick Ratio *[cash + marketable securities + accounts receivable] ÷ current liabilities*			
Days of Working Capital *([current assets - current liabilities] ÷ [total operating expense - depreciation expense]) × 365*			
Days of Cash on Hand *([cash + marketable securities] ÷ [total operating expense - depreciation expense]) × 365*			
Net Operating Income *revenue excess or deficiency ÷ expenses*			
Net Operating Ratio *net operating income ÷ total operating income*			
Dollars spent on administration and overhead			
amount (include all nonprogram costs):			
as a percentage of total assets:			
Funding Mix (indicate % of each type) Government:			
Foundation:			
Corporate:			
Individual donors:			
Earned income:			
Was an audit done?			

Are there written financial and administrative policies and procedures for this organization?   ☐ Yes   ☐ No

Human resource indicators

		Year			
Annual percentage turnover	Management staff:				
	Line staff:				
Average annual pay raise (percentage)	Management staff:				
	Line staff:				

Benefits offered

❏ Health insurance for employees

❏ Dental insurance for employees

❏ Health insurance for employees' dependents

❏ Dental insurance for employees' dependents

❏ Long-term disability insurance

❏ Life insurance

❏ Accidental death and dismemberment insurance

❏ Vision insurance

❏ Vacation time

❏ Flexible schedule

❏ Child care for employees' dependents

❏ 403(b) (or other) retirement savings plan (no employer contributions)

❏ Employer contributions to a 403(b) (or other) retirement savings plan

❏ Other: _____

❏ Other: _____

❏ Other: _____

❏ Other: _____

❏ Other: _____

Staff development policies (training, career development, etc.)

_____

_____

_____

_____

Are personnel policies and guidelines written down in any kind of formal document or manual?

_____

Do all employees get a copy of this manual? _____

Language Capacity (as related to service delivery)

Program / Service (break out if desired)	Language	# of people offering services in this language (FTE)

Average years of job-relevant experience _____

Use of Volunteers Year			
Number of Individual (non-board) Volunteers			
Total Volunteer Hours Contributed			

Governance Indicators

	Year			
Number of Board Members				
Annual percentage turnover of Board Members				
Number of meetings held annually				
Average attendance at board meetings				

Is there an assessment of the board's performance? _____

_____

_____

Is there a "board book" or other written set of guidelines for board members? _____

_____

Are minutes recorded and kept for each meeting? _____

_____

What offices are filled at the current time?

❑ President ❑ VP ❑ Secretary ❑ Treasurer ❑ Other (_____)

What standing committees exist? _____

_____

_____

Do you have an advisory board? ❑ Yes ❑ No   If yes, how large (# of members)? _____

How often does it meet? _____

_____

What other advisory bodies exist (if any)? _____

_____

_____

_____

Fundraising Indicators

	Year			
Number of fundraising staff (FTE)				
Cost of fundraising				
Number of major donors *(Major donor = contributes > $ _____)*				
Percent of board members donating money				
Total board contributions				

Does the agency have a written fundraising plan? _____

What types of fundraising does the organization do?

- ❑ Direct mail
- ❑ Personal solicitation
- ❑ Solicitation of planned gifts
- ❑ Special events
- ❑ Grant proposals
- ❑ Entrepreneurial ventures (selling client-made products, thrift store, etc.)
- ❑ Cause-related marketing arrangements with for-profit companies
- ❑ Other (please specify): _____

_____

_____

_____

_____

_____

Programmatic Indicators

Number of programs_____ Program	# of people served	Definition of a service unit	Total service units

Demographics: What types of people do you serve? Indicate using percentages in the blanks below.

Age	Annual Income	Ethnicity	Gender	Sexual Orientation
____ < 5	____ Poverty level or below	___ African American	____ Bisexual	____ Gay
____ 5 – 12	____ Low income	___ Asian American	____ Female	____ Lesbian
____ 13 – 18	____ Medium income	___ Caucasian	____ Male	____ Straight
____ 19 – 21	____ High income	___ European	____ Transgender	
____ 22 – 30		___ Hispanic / Latino		
____ 31 – 50		___ Native American		
____ 51 – 65		___ Pacific Islander		
____ > 65		___ Other: _____		
		___ Other: _____		
		___ Other: _____		
		___ Other: _____		

Do you keep track of how many client/patron complaints you get? ☐ Yes ☐ No

If yes, how many do you get per month (average)? _____

Do you keep track of client/patron turnover? ☐ Yes ☐ No

If yes, what is your turnover like now? _____

How do you measure success as an organization? _____

Do you use a scale? If so, what is it? _____

What is your current score on this measure? _____

Government Contract Performance Rating (if applicable): _____

The above questions may not all apply to all organizations. If this organization does work that cannot fairly be described or evaluated through the programmatic questions above, please write a few notes below that would be relevant. (For example, an arts organization might list size of collections, number of patrons/year, number of performances/year, growth in ticket sales, and so forth.)[10]

---

[10] We welcome suggestions for appropriate questions for organizations operating in different subsectors. Please direct all suggestions to info@lapiana.org.

Sample Ad for a Nonprofit Seeking a Partner

Chicago Nonprofit Looking for a Potential Partner

YouthFirst is a $2 million youth service organization serving greater Chicago. We offer after-school tutorial programs for children ages 6–13, vocational training for teenagers, a youth entrepreneurship program, and individual and group counseling services.

We are looking to expand our service offerings to cover entire families, and to reach out to a wider geographic area. Given the current funding environment, proven community need, and our desire to avoid duplicating services and "reinventing the wheel," we are looking to partner with— and perhaps to merge with—a like-minded organization.

What we offer:

- A solid 18-year history
- Expertise in youth-oriented programming
- Strong ties with the Chicago school system
- A diverse and committed board of directors
- Access to large donations of state-of-the-art technology

What we are looking for:

- Complementary program and skills
- Experience with family and elder care programming
- A geographic focus that includes but goes beyond inner-city Chicago
- A strong balance sheet and financial position
- Proven fundraising skills
- A passion for providing quality services to the community

If interested, please contact Erik Grueller at YouthFirst, 5555 N Main St, Anytown, IL 55555; (555) 555-6481.

Sample Confidentiality Agreement

CONFIDENTIALITY AGREEMENT by and between ABC and XYZ, nonprofit corporations incorporated in _____ and _____ .

ABC and XYZ are engaged in merger negotiations. As this process proceeds, sensitive, confidential, and/or proprietary information may be exchanged by the parties. In order to protect the privacy and business interests of each of the parties, they agree to the following terms:

1. At the conclusion of negotiations, if a merger is not agreed to, all copies of all documents distributed to each party or its agents by the other party or its agents will be returned to the originating party.

2. Neither party will at any time during the period of merger negotiations or after merger negotiations are concluded make known to any third party any information covered by this agreement or furnish any documents containing such information pertaining to the other party.

3. In the event a merger is not agreed upon, neither party will make any use or take advantage of anything it has learned about the other party's organization, board, staff, donors, clients, finances, legal dealings, or operations, nor will it use anything it has so learned to compete with the other party.

4. In the event a merger is not agreed upon, the parties will agree upon a joint statement to be issued to any third party requesting information about the merger negotiations. This statement will reflect positively upon both parties.

This agreement is entered into this _____ day of _____ , _____ .

_____   _____
Chairman of the Board, ABC   Chairman of the Board, XYZ

_____   _____
Executive Director, ABC   Executive Director, XYZ

Sample Implementation/ Integration Plan

For the merger of: __ABC and XYZ__

(Note: This plan assumes that both boards have passed resolutions committing to a merger of the two organizations at the earliest possible date.)

Implementation

1. Retain a lawyer to oversee the legal process of merging ABC and XYZ. Work with the lawyer as he or she:

   - Reviews the proposed merger agreement and makes any recommendations with regard to legality, appropriateness, compliance with all federal and state laws, and other pertinent details.

   - Verifies that the chosen legal method of merger is the most appropriate. If the negotiations committee and boards did *not* choose a method, the lawyer should make a recommendation as to the best method.

   - Proposes and/or reviews any necessary changes to the bylaws of any surviving corporations.

   - Makes any recommendations with regard to union issues, union negotiations, and related issues. (Note: An attorney specializing in labor law may be needed if union issues are involved.)

   - Files for a tax clearance certificate for any dissolving corporations.

   - Files the appropriate paperwork to merge the corporations.

2. While waiting for the legal papers to be filed and take effect, form an implementation steering committee and begin planning for integration. (See below.)

Integration

Board Integration

Task	Lead person(s)	Time Frame[11]
Decide if the organizations would like to create interlocking boards while waiting for the legal process to take effect. If yes: • Decide which individuals will be on the new board. • Check the bylaws of the merging organizations for any restrictions with regard to the number of board members allowed. If a change is needed to any organization's bylaws, that organization should vote to make the change. • Each organization should nominate and vote onto its board the individuals selected to be on the new board. This may require that some existing board members step down. • Proceed with the steps below. If no, proceed with the steps below.	Boards of the merging organizations	Prior to agreement—Month 1
If not already specified by the negotiations committee, select the individuals who will make up the executive committee of the new board.	Negotiations committee *or* boards of the merging organizations	Month 1
Form an implementation steering committee. This is typically made up of the nominated executive director (if one has been chosen) for the merged entity, and those individuals who will make up the executive committee of the new board. Many others will be involved in implementation, but this group will work with the future board to lead the efforts.	Boards of the merging organizations	Month 1

[11] The notations given in the "Lead Person" and "Time Frame" columns are for guidance only. Each merger presents unique challenges and demands. The time frame for each step, for example, will vary according to the number and size of the organizations involved, the presence or lack of an executive director for the merged entity at the beginning of the integration process, the cultural differences between the merging organizations, and the degree to which the board and staff are able to devote sufficient time to the integration process in the crucial early months.

The time values in the "Time Frame" column indicate in which month *after* the approval of the merger agreement the activity is typically addressed. "Month 1" indicates that the activity is done within the first month after the agreement is approved, "Month 2" indicates that the activity is done within the second month after the agreement is approved, and so forth.

Task	Lead person(s)	Time Frame
Hold a meeting of the implementation steering committee. 1. If an executive director has not yet been chosen, plan for and begin the search and hiring process. Options: internal search/decision; external search/decision; retain executive search service. 2. Discuss procedures and expectations for the new board. 3. Plan a retreat or meeting for the nominated members of the new board. 4. Create an initial budget for implementation and integration. Begin planning for any necessary fundraising efforts.	Implementation steering committee	Months 1–2
Survey the nominated members of the new board with regard to committee interests.	Implementation steering committee	Months 1–2
Hold a retreat or meeting for the nominated members of the new board.	Implementation steering committee	Month 1 or 2
Continue regular meetings of the nominated members of the new board until the merger has become legal, and that group *is* the board of directors for the merged organization.	Implementation steering committee	Until merger has become legal, typically 2–4 months
Engage in strategic planning for the merged organization. Clarify mission/vision, goals/objectives, internal and environmental analysis, and means for future evaluation of progress.	New board, with executive director and senior staff	Months 4–17
Create and revise over time a budget for the merged organization, based on the work of the negotiations committee, the implementation steering committee, any strategic planning done by the new board, and the results of management team and systems integration planning. (See sections below.)	Executive director, with new board	Month 1 and onward; to be revised continually as planning is done

Management Integration

Task	Lead person(s)	Time Frame
Finalize selection of the executive director, if this has not already been done.	Negotiations committee *or* new board	Prior to agreement—Month 2
Clarify the executive director's responsibilities and authority prior to the full legal implementation of the merger. Formalize any management agreements desired by the organizations.	Negotiations committee *or* boards of the merging organizations	Month 1

Task	Lead person(s)	Time Frame
Decide on the parameters for a management team. This can involve specifying what positions are necessary, or simply how much money is available in the budget for the executive director to spend on a management team.	Executive director, with new board	Prior to agreement— Months 1–2
Decide which of the current employees (of the pre-merger organizations) can best fill the management team positions.	Executive director, with appropriate senior staff	Prior to agreement— Months 1–2
Decide what, if any, layoffs will be needed among current employees at the management level.	Executive director, with appropriate senior staff	Prior to agreement— Months 1–2
Decide what, if any, severance package(s) will be offered to departing employees.	Executive director, with board review and approval	Prior to agreement— Months 1–2
Announce the composition of the management team and all necessary job losses at the same time.	Executive director	Months 1–2
Hold a meeting of the new management team.	Executive director	Months 1–2
Work with management team to evaluate staffing and plan for staff integration.	Executive director	Months 1–2

Staff Integration

Task	Lead person(s)	Time Frame
Decide what staffing changes will need to be made in order to integrate the organizations. Decide what, if any, layoffs will be needed among current employees.	Executive director, with management team	Month 2
Decide what, if any, severance package(s) will be offered to departing staff.	Executive director, with management team, with board review and approval	Month 2
Announce all necessary job losses among staff at the same time.	Executive director, with management team	Month 2

Task	Lead person(s)	Time Frame
Begin the process of integrating staff from the pre-merger organizations: 1. Plan and hold a staff retreat, social event, and/or series of socially-oriented meetings to celebrate the merger and facilitate staff from different organizations getting to know one another. 2. Form cross-functional teams to develop and propose solutions to systems integration issues. (See below.) 3. Organize site visits and work teams among staff with analogous roles. 4. Combine the training and staff development functions of the two former organizations. 5. If the merging organizations had staff working at dispersed sites, attempt, to the extent possible, to shift offices and move people around to bring staff from the different organizations together, and begin reducing the sense of completely separate organizations.	Executive director, with management team	Months 1–12
Ensure continuing opportunities for information flow, communication, and the prompt identification of conflict and concerns among staff.	Executive director, with management team	Ongoing
Ensure continuing attention to the development of a new, merged culture, as well as to culture clash.	Executive director, with management team	Ongoing

Systems Integration

Task	Lead person(s)	Time Frame
Identify the systems needing integration, both immediately and long-term. • Accounting system • Budgeting process • Payroll system • Human resource management systems • Information systems • Purchasing processes • Inventory and control systems • Bidding and major equipment maintenance schedules • Risk management policies and processes • Annual calendar of donor events, solicitations, and other fundraising • Strategic planning and monitoring processes • Outcome measurement systems	Executive director, with management team and implementation steering committee	Months 1–2

Task	Lead person(s)	Time Frame
For each area needing integration, form a team to review current systems and develop recommendations for integration. The teams should be made up of staff from each of the merging organizations whenever possible.	Management team and staff	Month 2
Hire any consultants or experts necessary to assist with the review and recommendation process.	Management team, with executive director	Month 2
Plan a time line for systems integration, ensuring that the necessary budgetary resources are in place or being sought to cover the costs. Identify actions needed in the short-term, medium-term, and long-term.	Management team, with executive director	Month 2
Proceed with integration, using staff, management, and outside consultants or experts as necessary.	Management team and staff, with executive director review	Ongoing
Continue regular check-ins with staff and management to ensure that systems integration is progressing as planned, and is meeting the needs of the merged organization.	Management team, with executive director	Ongoing

Communications and Public Relations

Task	Lead person(s)	Time Frame
Make a public announcement of the merger. This can be done at any point after the boards involved have voted to move forward with the merger, depending on the goals and wishes of the organizations.	Executive director, new board	Month 1
Plan for and hold a public event celebrating the merger. Use it to introduce the merged organization to donors, funders, clients, and the greater community.	Executive director, communications staff	Months 2–4
Offer updates on the merger and the implementation process in any newsletters, publications, etc. that are put out.	Executive director, communications staff	Ongoing
If the merged organization's name is not yet chosen, and public input is desired, plan for and announce a means for gathering input and making a decision with regard to the new name. Announce and celebrate any name change.	Executive director, new board	Within first year

Resource List

Amherst H. Wilder Foundation. *Nonprofit Decline and Dissolution Project Report*. Minneapolis: Amherst Wilder Foundation, 1989.

> This 1987 study reports on the decline and dissolution of nonprofit organizations, distills warning signs, internal and external causes, management and governance strategies, and community and funder reactions for nonprofits considering dissolution.

Arsenault, Jane. *Forging Nonprofit Alliances: A Comprehensive Guide to Enhancing Your Mission through Joint Ventures and Partnerships, Management Service Organizations, Parent Corporations, and Mergers*. San Francisco: Jossey-Bass, 1998.

> This book shows how nonprofit organizations can use consolidation as a strategic tool to enhance their mission. The author explores options for consolidation, details negotiation processes, and suggests how to make the experience positive and constructive for staff, board members, donors, and constituents. The book includes worksheets, examples, and sample documents.

Bolman, Lee G. and Terrence E. Deal. "Merger Meltdown," *Healthcare Forum Journal*, 1994, November-December.

> The authors describe recent merger trends in health care organizations. Of interest to the nonprofit sector are the authors' cautionary remarks on why health care organizations must pay more attention to the human element in merger transactions to prevent the well-publicized human resources disasters recorded during and after for-profit corporate mergers and acquisitions.

Bryson, John M. *Strategic Planning for Public and Nonprofit Organizations.* San Francisco: Jossey-Bass, 1995.

First published in 1988 and reprinted nine times, this classic work by John Bryson has become a standard in the public and nonprofit sectors. The author shows how nonprofit leaders can use strategic planning to strengthen organizations and emphasizes the importance of participants in any effort to "think and act strategically."

"Consolidation: A Nonprofit Success Story," *Nonprofit World*, 1989, March/April, Vol. 7, No. 2, 20-22.

This story of the consolidation of two Alaskan nonprofit organizations exemplifies how nonprofits can and often should pursue consolidation from a perspective of strength, while they are "ahead" rather than when they find themselves in organizational trouble.

Ernst, David. "Coffee and One Way to Boston," *The McKinsey Quarterly*, 1996, No. 1, 165-175.

The authors present current partnership and alliance options available to for-profit organizations. The article includes cautionary advice to interested parties. Of interest to nonprofits is the article's abundance of externally-oriented strategies that are common in the for-profit world. When adapted to the needs and characteristics of nonprofits, these can be of strategic value.

Fenn, Donna. "The New Dog-Eat-Dog Nonprofit," *Information Access Company*, 1995, July, Vol. 17, No. 10, 1-5.

This article describes how a Missouri nonprofit organization flourished by adopting management strategies traditionally used in the for-profit world, such as customer service and relationship marketing. Between 1990 and 1994, contributions rose by 36 percent and earned revenues grew by 152 percent.

Greater New York Fund/United Way. *Merger: Another Path Ahead.* New York: Greater New York Fund, 1981.

This 1981 guide to the nonprofit merger process is one of the earliest works in strategic restructuring. It offers a rationale for considering merger, several decision-making checklists for the exploring parties, and step-by-step advice on the merger process. The guide contains real-world examples and a legal appendix.

Hodgkin, Christopher. "What You Should Know About Nonprofit Mergers," *Nonprofit World*, 1994, July/August, 4-5.

This article briefly describes important legal issues to consider when two nonprofit organizations explore merger.

Kerr, Christine. "Human Resourcing Following a Merger," *Information Access Company*, 1996, September, Vol. 34, No. 5, 1-3.

> This article examines human resource strategies adopted during and after the merger of HSBC Holdings PLC and Midland Bank in 1992. Some of the human resource strategies shown in this article may be of use to nonprofit leaders during and after a merger. Applicable strategies for nonprofits are those that are not inherent to the mission of for-profit organizations.

"Keys to a Successful Nonprofit Merger," *Nonprofit World*, 1992, May/June, Vol. 10, No. 3, 14-18.

> This case study of a nonprofit merger offers step-by-step advice and evidence of successful transactions during a merger.

Kibbe, Barbara and Fred Setterberg. *Succeeding with Consultants: Self-Assessment for the Changing Nonprofit.* The David and Lucile Packard Foundation, 1992.

> Written for nonprofit executives and board members, this book provides practical advice on selecting and utilizing consultants. It covers a wide array of topics; highlights situations where a consultant might be valuable; suggests ways to find, hire, and work with consultants; and provides valuable self-assessment tools to help nonprofits identify their organizational strengths and weaknesses.

Kreidler, John. "Leverage Lost: The Nonprofit Arts in the Post-Ford Era." Circulated in manuscript, version dated March 16, 1996.

> The author paints a bleak picture for nonprofit arts organizations in the United States as the twentieth century comes to an end. This environment of scarcity poses an ideal opportunity for nonprofit arts organizations to consider strategic restructuring as a strategy to survive and succeed.

La Piana, David. *Beyond Collaboration: Strategic Restructuring of Nonprofit Organizations.* Revised Edition. Washington, D.C.: National Center for Nonprofit Boards and San Francisco: The James Irvine Foundation, 1998.

> This 1996 study analyzes current strategic restructuring efforts among nonprofit organizations and describes strategies funders can develop to support and encourage partnering in the nonprofit sector. It also highlights nonprofit organizations' needs in the area of organizational change while pointing at research gaps in strategic restructuring.

La Piana, David. "Forging a Successful Merger," *The Nonprofit Times*, July, 1993.

> This article highlights misconceptions nonprofit leaders have about mergers, describes characteristics of successful nonprofit mergers, and offers warnings to those engaged in the process. Finally, the article discusses the rationale for nonprofit mergers and the power embedded in them.

La Piana, David. "Is Your Organization a Candidate for Strategic Restructuring?," *The Not-for-Profit CEO Monthly Letter*, 1997, December, Vol. 5, No. 2, 1-3.

This article guides nonprofit leaders to the discovery of opportunities that exist in strategic restructuring as well as the risks that are involved. It also highlights the different options available to nonprofits in strategic restructuring as well as major roadblocks that can be encountered in the process.

La Piana, David. *Nonprofit Mergers: The Board's Responsibility to Consider the Unthinkable.* Washington, D.C.: National Center for Nonprofit Boards, 1994.

This booklet is a practical step-by-step guide for nonprofit leaders who are considering, exploring, or engaging in the merger process. The author offers advice to nonprofit managers and board members as well as a list of recommended readings.

Lewis, Fritz C. and Charles R. Chandler. "The Urge to Merge: A Common Sense Approach to Association Consolidation," *Association Management*, March 1993, 81-84.

This article recounts the story of a successful merger between two previously competing associations. The authors were the former chief executive officers of the two groups. One author became the chief executive officer of the new group; the other became the chief operating officer.

McLaughlin, Thomas A. "Giving Diligence Its Due: Financially Tricky Situations Arise in Mergers," *The Nonprofit Times,* October, 1996.

McLaughlin, Thomas A. "How to Consider Forming Alliances: There are Many Forms of Successful, Mutual Co-existence," *The Nonprofit Times,* November, 1995.

McLaughlin, Thomas A. *Nonprofit Mergers and Alliances: A Strategic Planning Guide.* New York: Wiley & Sons, 1998.

Using real-world examples and case studies, this book offers clear, practical, step-by-step guidance through the nonprofit merger process. Focusing on issues of concern to nonprofit leaders, McLaughlin discusses the context in which nonprofit mergers and alliances take place as well as the forces that shape the use of strategic restructuring options.

McLaughlin, Thomas A. *Seven Steps to a Successful Nonprofit Merger.* Washington, D.C.: National Center for Nonprofit Boards, 1996.

An overview of a comprehensive process developed to assist nonprofit organizations in implementing a merger. Explains what steps should be taking in what order, with helpful tips along the way.

McLaughlin, Thomas A. "Why Mergers Fail: Here's What to Do About It," *The Nonprofit Times,* April, 1998.

McMurtry, Steven L., F. Ellen Netting, and Peter M. Kettner. "How Nonprofits Adapt to a Stringent Environment," *Nonprofit Management and Leadership*, 1991, Vol. 1, No. 3, 235-252.

This article reviews the decline of human service organizations in Arizona and the strategies they take to combat diminishing resources. It provides the context within which to consider merger, but does not specifically describe the merger process.

O'Brien, J. and P. Collier. "Merger Problems for Human Service Agencies: A Case Study." *Administration in Social Work*, 1991, Vol. 15, No. 3, 19-31.

This article reports some of the trouble spots encountered by merging human service organizations highlighting culture clash and systems integration issues. It argues for tending to the often overlooked human issues found throughout the merger process. The article does not focus on issues related to self-interest and autonomy.

O'Connell, Brian. *Board Overboard: Laughs and Lessons for All but the Perfect Nonprofit.* San Francisco: Jossey-Bass, 1995.

O'Connell is the founding president of Independent Sector, a national coalition of voluntary and philanthropic organizations. In this book, presented in the form of one organization's board meeting minutes, he spoofs typical board behavior.

Salipante, Paul F., and Karen Golden-Bibble. "Managing Traditionality and Strategic Change in Nonprofit Organizations," *Nonprofit Management and Leadership*, 1995, Vol. 6, No. 1, 3-20.

This article examines and promotes the retention of organizational traditions in nonprofits as an internal management strategy for maintaining continuity. It warns of the risks of externally-focused organizational change strategies, which it characterizes as inappropriate to nonprofit groups because of the possibility of disruption in time-tested organizational practices. The authors argue that surviving and succeeding in a turbulent environment is already disruptive enough for nonprofit groups.

Singer, Mark I., and John A. Yankey. "Organizational Metamorphosis: A Study of Eighteen Nonprofit Mergers, Acquisitions and Consolidations." *Nonprofit Management and Leadership*, 1995, Vol. 1, No. 4, 357-369.

After reviewing the literature on nonprofit mergers and studying eighteen cases of various nonprofit consolidation transactions, the authors point at financial reasons as the main motivation for the nonprofit mergers studied. They cite small nonprofits' inability to compete as a common rationale for considering merger. The authors go on to describe changes in staff morale and productivity and point out leadership and communication as vital factors in the success of nonprofit mergers.

Taylor, J., M. J. Austin, and R. K. Caputo. "Managing Mergers of Human Service Agencies: People, Programs, and Procedures." *Child Welfare*, 1992, Vol. 71, No. 1, 37-52.

This article studies sixteen small-to-large social service agency mergers. Describing steps in the merger process, the article presents guidelines that may be of use to agencies exploring consolidation.

"The Power of Mergers: Finding New Energy through Mission-Based Restructuring," *Board Member*. Washington, D.C.: National Center for Nonprofit Boards, 1997, Vol. 6, No. 8, 1-16.

This special edition newsletter highlights factors that drive nonprofits to consider strategic restructuring, roadblocks to strategic restructuring, and key steps in the merger process. The issue includes several useful case studies of nonprofits that have used strategic restructuring.

Unterman, Israel, and Richard H. Davis. *Strategic Management of Not-for-Profit Organizations: From Survival to Success*. New York: Praeger, 1984.

In this nonprofit management classic, a cadre of nonprofit management experts describe how nonprofit leaders can enhance their management strategies and move from survival to success in their day-to-day operations. The authors emphasize the strategic value of cross-sector partnerships between nonprofit and for-profit corporations.

Wernet, Stephen P., and Sandra A. Jones. "Merger and Acquisition Activity Between Nonprofit Social Service Organizations: A Case Study," *Nonprofit and Voluntary Sector Quarterly*, Winter 1992, Vol. 21, No. 4, 367-380.

This early study of a merger between two nonprofit social service organizations is described within a for-profit context of mergers and acquisitions. The authors describe the process and content of merger transactions and the interactions between the various stakeholders. Attention is given to events surrounding the process and to costs and rewards to stakeholders.

Wolfred, Tim. *Leadership Lost: Report on an ED Tenure Study*. San Francisco: The Support Center for Nonprofit Management/Nonprofit Development Center, 1999.

The author surveyed 137 executive directors regarding their future career plans. He reports finding a high percentage (66 percent) who are in their first executive director job, and a startlingly low percentage (25 percent) who would pursue a second such job.

Yankey, John A. and Mark L. Singer. "Managing Mergers and Consolidations," in R. Edward and J. Yankey (Eds) *Skills for Effective Human Services Management*, Silver Spring, MD: NASW Press, 1990.

This article offers nonprofit leaders an update on merger and consolidation best practices. The authors define restructuring options and offer tips on partnership exploration and implementation, a case study, and a skills exercise for nonprofit leaders considering merger or consolidation.

Worksheets

In practice, the motivation to consider a merger may stem from several factors, and these factors may overlap to some degree. What motivates your organization to consider a merger? Note that motivators are more general in nature than the specific outcomes you desire from the merger. (These are covered in the next worksheet.)

1.

2.

3.

4.

Which of the three elements of the *Strategic Motivations Mix* (improving finances, gaining access to a larger skill set, or enhancing your pursuit of mission) best describes your own motivations, as expressed above? Is more than one type of motivator operating?

Our highest priority outcomes for the merger are:

1.

   How will we measure accomplishment of this outcome?

2.

   How will we measure accomplishment of this outcome?

Published by the Amherst H. Wilder Foundation   Copyright © 2000 David La Piana

continued

3.

How will we measure accomplishment of this outcome?

4.

How will we measure accomplishment of this outcome?

Published by the Amherst H. Wilder Foundation   Copyright © 2000 David La Piana

As a group, recount your organization's mission statement. (It's okay to look it up if no one can remember it.)

Hopefully the essence of the statement can fit in the space provided. The shorter it is, the better. An overly long mission statement is sure to include information better articulated somewhere else. Moreover, the longer the mission statement, the less likely it is that anyone will be able to commit it to memory, which means that it will have limited usefulness.

Now rewrite the statement, deleting all references to services, programs, or how the mission is accomplished. Sometimes a clause will begin with the word "by" or "through," as in the statement "The Community Center is committed to ending poverty in our neighborhood, *through the provision of health and social services.*" For this exercise you would delete the second half of the sentence, beginning with the word "through."

You should now have boiled down your mission statement to its essence: a statement of what the organization is trying to accomplish. If it turns out that in following these instructions you deleted the entire mission statement (or close to it), then your mission statement is probably focused too much on service provision, and not enough on outcome. Try writing a new statement; one that contains no references to services or programs, and thus passes the above test.

Published by the Amherst H. Wilder Foundation   Copyright © 2000 David La Piana

continued

This restatement of your mission is what should be carried into discussions with your potential partner. If both organizations go through this exercise it will be easier to avoid getting stuck in a "mission rut" during negotiations. Instead of taking a stand in support of their beloved (and very specific) mission *statements* (a situation which can cause conflict over relatively minor wording differences), both organizations will be more open to discussing how the essence of their missions can best be advanced. It is this essence that is really each organization's reason for existence, after all, and it is more likely to be compatible with that of the other organization than a more specific, service-oriented statement.

The wordsmithing of the mission statement for the new (merged) organization can now be an attempt to incorporate the essence of the two original missions into one statement—a statement that still does not focus on programs.

List the top three critical issues facing your nonprofit, from the perspectives of the board, executive, management staff, and line staff. *Critical issues* are defined as those issues that are most significant to the organization's future success. These are the issues you *must* address. Don't make the mistake of guessing what each constituency thinks. Survey them, ask them in person, call a sample of people on the phone. Regardless of the outcome of the merger considerations, this exercise will be useful in that it will help you to identify the priorities and perspectives of crucial internal constituencies.

Board of directors

1. _____

2. _____

3. _____

Executive director

1. _____

2. _____

3. _____

Management staff

1. _____

2. _____

3. _____

Line staff

1. _____

2. _____

3. _____

Are there major differences in the critical issues identified by the different groups? Are the issues complementary or competing?

Survey members of each of your four primary internal constituencies about their reaction to the merger opportunity you are currently considering. Once again, don't make the mistake of guessing what each constituency thinks. Survey them, ask them in person, call a sample of people on the phone. If you decide to go forward with a merger, it will be important to both understand these constituent viewpoints, and ensure that everyone in your organization "speaks with one voice" throughout the process.

After discussion, rate each constituency's reaction to the following statements. (You may either list all responses in the chart below, or average the responses to each statement for each constituency.)

1	2	3	4	5
Strongly Agree	Agree	Neutral	Disagree	Strongly Disagree

	Board of Directors	Executive Director	Management Staff	Line Staff
1. A merger with this partner is a good idea.				
2. I feel good about this process.				
3. I look forward to staying on after the merger.				
4. I will support the board's decision whether I agree or not.				
5. Mergers are the wave of the future in our field.				

Any rating above a 3, if expressed by a significant number of individuals from any constituency, is cause for concern. Try to determine what is behind any negative feelings. Is it lack of information? Fear of the unknown? Dislike of the other group?

Can the negativity be addressed and remedied by fostering greater familiarity with the other group? Through joint meetings or joint task forces? Through better communication about the identified motivators, desired outcomes, or the process?

Published by the Amherst H. Wilder Foundation   Copyright © 2000 David La Piana

Answer the following questions as honestly as possible:

	Yes	No
1. Do members of our board of directors and our executive director get along?	☐	☐
2. Do they respect one another?	☐	☐
3. Do they routinely support one another?	☐	☐
4. Are disagreements and differences discussed openly and respectfully?	☐	☐
5. Think back to the last major decision the organization made; a decision big enough to involve both the board and the executive director. Did the way this decision was made exemplify board-management rapport, respect, and mutual support?	☐	☐

6. Who is really "in charge" at our nonprofit?

Is the board satisfied with this arrangement?

Is the executive director satisfied with this arrangement?

Are other staff members satisfied with this arrangement?

7. Has the organization experienced high turnover in executive directors? (Say more than once every four years)

8. Do board members tend to leave before their term is over?

Are you currently facing a crisis in your organization? There are many types of crises: an acute cash shortage, the unexpected departure of one or more key executives, the ramifications of huge or sudden growth, a public relations debacle, a major internal power struggle, and so forth. As a board, think about your organization's situation, and write down what crises (if any) you are facing right now.

1.

2.

3.

Will you be able to resolve these crises before entering into merger discussions with another party? If not, how will they affect the process? Think both about how they will weaken your position, and how you might be able to compensate for this, or use it as an impetus to make changes in your organization.

Published by the Amherst H. Wilder Foundation   Copyright © 2000 David La Piana

Are you successful risk-takers? Recount three risky endeavors you undertook successfully.

1.

2.

3.

Are there other times when your organization undertook great risks, but did *not* succeed? What factors led to this lack of success?

Was your organization more or less likely to take risks after these occasions?

Given its experiences with success and failure, how is your organization likely to respond to a merger?

What has been the percentage growth of your annual operating budget during each of the past five years, relative to the year immediately preceding? Express downsizing as a negative number (for example, express a 10% budget reduction as -10%).

	Year	Percentage Growth
This year over last year (/)		
Last year over the previous year (/)		
That year over the previous year (/)		
That year over the previous year (/)		
That year over the previous year (/)		
What do you anticipate to be the percentage growth of your annual operating budget for the next year?		

                                                                    Yes   No

1. Does your organization welcome growth?   ☐   ☐

    Give an example: _____

    _____

    _____

    _____

2. Are your systems easily expandable to accommodate growth?   ☐   ☐

    Give an example: _____

    _____

    _____

    _____

3. Does your board have a plan for incorporating new members?   ☐   ☐

    Give an example: _____

    _____

    _____

    _____

This worksheet is best completed by each organization separately, prior to the start of negotiations. Once the negotiation process is underway, both parties can share their answers to this worksheet with the other, and together they can discuss how their ideas regarding choosing a leader might be compatible and how any differences could be resolved.

Indicate all of the acceptable ways to resolve the question of who will lead the merged organization:

❏ Our current executive director takes the helm of the merged organization.

❏ Our partner's current executive director takes the helm of the merged organization.

❏ We ask the two incumbents to recommend which one of them should serve as the executive.

❏ Another staff person within one of the organizations takes the helm of the merged organization.

❏ The two boards hold a joint selection process and decide between the two current executive directors.

❏ The two boards hold a joint selection process and decide between the two current executive directors *and* outside candidates.

❏ The merged board chooses an executive director through a post-merger selection process.

❏ _____

❏ _____

❏ _____

❏ _____

❏ _____

❏ _____

❏ _____

❏ _____

❏ _____

❏ _____

❏ _____

❏ _____

❏ _____

❏ _____

❏ _____

Record or identify stories of successful nonprofit mergers in your community or within your field. Is everyone in your organization aware of these success stories? If not, share them. They may prove inspirational, or at least reassuring, to those who are not clear on what a merger means or how it could be implemented.

Published by the Amherst H. Wilder Foundation

What level of trust exists between your organization and your potential partner?
We will refer to this number as your "trust score."

1	2	3	4	5
Distrust	Low trust	Moderate trust	High trust	Inadequate opportunity to build trust

List five experiences that have influenced the feelings of trust or distrust that led to
your selection of a trust score.

1.

2.

3.

4.

5.

If your selection of a trust score was based on fewer than five incidents it might indicate that your view of your potential partner is colored more by feeling than reality.

List five ways in which you have worked with this particular potential partner in the past. Rate your overall satisfaction with each experience.

1.

| Totally Dissatisfied | Not Satisfied | Neutral | Satisfied | Very Satisfied |

2.

| Totally Dissatisfied | Not Satisfied | Neutral | Satisfied | Very Satisfied |

3.

| Totally Dissatisfied | Not Satisfied | Neutral | Satisfied | Very Satisfied |

continued

4.

Totally Dissatisfied	Not Satisfied	Neutral	Satisfied	Very Satisfied

5.

Totally Dissatisfied	Not Satisfied	Neutral	Satisfied	Very Satisfied

If you have a somewhat negative opinion of your potential partner but have less than five experiences listed here, it could be that your opinion is based more on the subjective than the objective. If this is the case, try to learn more about this organization. Face-to-face discussions can help to build a positive relationship where in the past absence and distance may have bred negativity.

Make a list of what you believe to be the greatest assets of your potential partner. Then take out Worksheets 2 and 4 and study your lists of desired outcomes and critical issues. Which of your potential partner's skills and assets would help you achieve your desired outcomes, address your critical issues, or both? Under what conditions would those skills and assets truly be usable for your organization?

Your potential partner's skills/assets:	What desired outcome (D.O.) or critical issue (C.I.) is addressed by this skill/asset?	How is this skill/asset usable to you?

Published by the Amherst H. Wilder Foundation   Copyright © 2000 David La Piana

Ask members of the board, staff, and management team to describe the fears and concerns they have about loss of autonomy for the organization, its programs, or its people. Discuss each issue thoroughly, attempting to clarify misunderstandings, create compromises, and articulate the advantages to be gained in exchange for a lesser degree of autonomy. If you prefer, recreate the worksheet on a flip chart for group use.

Fear or Concern	Response or Compensating gain from merger

continued

Fear or Concern	Response or Compensating gain from merger

Ask members of the board, staff, and management teams to answer the following questions:

- In what ways are your personal interests threatened by this partnership?
- What would help you to feel less threatened and more secure in moving forward?

As a group, complete the left-hand column, including the initials of any individual who is affected by a particular concern. Then return to the right-hand column and try to discover what steps the organizations could take to provide reassurance or clarification of each person's concern.

Who	Fear or Concern	Reassurance or Clarification sought

continued

Who	Fear or Concern	Reassurance or Clarification sought

Published by the Amherst H. Wilder Foundation   Copyright © 2000 David La Piana

Describe your organization's values, its heroes, and its cherished customs. Tell one story that is important in your organization's history. Discuss your completed worksheets with your potential partner to get a feel for the subtleties of the other's culture. Remember, much of what makes up an organization's culture is unspoken, but it is very much present and alive.

Our organization's values include:

1. _____

   _____

2. _____

   _____

3. _____

   _____

4. _____

   _____

5. _____

   _____

Our heroes are:

1. _____

   _____

2. _____

   _____

3. _____

   _____

4. _____

   _____

5. _____

   _____

continued

Some of our most cherished customs are:

1. _____
   _____

2. _____
   _____

3. _____
   _____

4. _____
   _____

5. _____
   _____

Tell a story that is important to your organization.

This questionnaire is a way of gauging staff's understanding of and feelings about the merger our organization is contemplating. It will take only a few minutes to complete and will give us a good overview of your concerns, which will then be discussed at an all-staff meeting. Please understand that your responses will be both anonymous and confidential. The completed form should be returned directly to our consultant in the envelope provided. The consultant will then analyze the responses and develop a report, which will be shared with you and our board of directors. The actual questionnaires will then be destroyed.

1. Name of organization _____

2. Years with the organization ☐ 0-1 ☐ 2-3 ☐ 4-8 ☐ 9+

3. Describe your understanding of the reasons a merger is being considered.

4. What is your opinion of your potential merger partner (the other organization)?

☐ Very positive ☐ Positive ☐ Neutral, no opinion ☐ Negative ☐ Very negative

5. What is your worst fear about the merger, should it occur?

6. What is your greatest hope for the merger, should it occur?

7. Please feel free to tell us anything else you think about this proposed merger. Feel free to use the back of this page if you need more room.

Fill in the chart below, using check marks to indicate that a statement is true for a given organization.

	Corporation 1:	Corporation 2:	Corporation 3:
The corporation has a license or certification that would be very difficult to obtain or transfer (e.g., FQHC – Federally Qualified Health Center).			
The corporation has significant debt which must be repaid if it dissolves because the creditor is unwilling to transfer the obligation to a different entity.			
The corporation has a funding source that is unwilling to transfer the funding to a new entity.			
The corporation was created by statute and requires governmental action to dissolve.			
The corporation is a membership organization and the members will not approve the dissolution of the corporation.			

The more check marks an organization has under its name, the less likely it is that it should be the dissolving corporation. This worksheet should help make clear that the choice of who "survives" and who dissolves is not a matter of winning and losing but instead depends on practical considerations.

Indicate which assets your corporation wishes to transfer (or acquire), and their approximate value. Each asset may be exchanged for cash, or for an agreement to preserve and protect it, or for further consideration. Fill in the type of exchange under the heading "Method of payment."

Note: if the transferring 501(c)(3) corporation is distributing all or substantially all of its assets, or if the sale is to anything but another public charity (regardless of the size of the sale), stop and seek legal counsel before you proceed. These transactions, if handled improperly, can bring serious negative tax consequences, including the payment of taxes and penalties or the possible loss of the organization's tax exemption.

Name of organization *from* which
these assets would be transferred: _____

Name of organization *to* which
these assets would be transferred: _____

Description of asset	Approximate value	Method of payment

TOTAL _____

Use this worksheet to help you design an interlocking board. As a first step, list the names of all current members of each board of directors.

Org Name: _____   Org Name: _____

1. _____	1. _____
2. _____	2. _____
3. _____	3. _____
4. _____	4. _____
5. _____	5. _____
6. _____	6. _____
7. _____	7. _____
8. _____	8. _____
9. _____	9. _____
10. _____	10. _____
11 _____	11. _____
12. _____	12. _____
13. _____	13. _____
14. _____	14. _____
15. _____	15. _____
16. _____	16. _____
17. _____	17. _____
18. _____	18. _____
19. _____	19. _____
20. _____	20. _____
21. _____	21. _____
22. _____	22. _____
23. _____	23. _____
24. _____	24. _____
25. _____	25. _____

Published by the Amherst H. Wilder Foundation   Copyright © 2000 David La Piana

continued

Now determine how many slots the newly constituted boards will have. In order to avoid creating an unwieldy board you may need to reduce the total number of board slots. For example, if there are 24 board members, you may want to create interlocking boards with a total of 12 members, 6 from each group. List below the names of those board members who will continue on to serve as members of the boards of both organizations. At their respective board meetings, ask each organization to elect this group as its board.

Board of *Both* Organizations

1. _____   16. _____

2. _____   17. _____

3. _____   18. _____

4. _____   19. _____

5. _____   20. _____

6. _____   21. _____

7. _____   22. _____

8. _____   23. _____

9. _____   24. _____

10. _____   25. _____

11. _____   26. _____

12. _____   27. _____

13. _____   28. _____

14. _____   29. _____

15. _____   30. _____

Develop three new traditions that will be unique to the merged nonprofit. A tradition is anything that involves a large number of employees, is fun, and can be repeated. It could be an annual holiday party, a staff appreciation day, a softball team, or something as simple as having food at all staff meetings. Resist the urge to import traditions from the old organizations. Develop some traditions that are completely new, or at least adapted with a significant new twist.

New Traditions:

1.

2.

3.

Develop two stories about the new organization. Tell them at staff meetings, and encourage their spread to new employees as they are hired. An appropriate story could be a funny incident that occurred during the merger negotiations, a misunderstanding caused by the cultural differences of the organizations (and then cleared up), or a battle fought (and won) with a funder who was reluctant to transfer a contract from one group to the other. The stories should express an insider's perspective, pride in the nonprofit, a sense of the organization's uniqueness, a commitment to excellence, or esprit de corps.

New Stories:

1.

2.

Legal	Nonprofit Attorney		_____
	Optional Specialists:	Labor specialist	_____
		Business litigation specialist	_____
		Real estate specialist	_____
		Antitrust specialist	_____

Consultants	Merger Consultant/Facilitator		_____
	Optional Specialists:	MIS specialist	_____
		Finance specialist	_____
		Human Resource specialist	_____

Design and Printing	Logo Design	_____
	Printing	_____
	Signage	_____

Severance
1. Weekly Salary_____ x ____weeks + fringe _____ = _____
2. Weekly Salary_____ x ____weeks + fringe _____ = _____
3. Weekly Salary_____ x ____weeks + fringe _____ = _____
4. Weekly Salary_____ x ____weeks + fringe _____ = _____

Outplacement Counseling   _____

Moving	Professional Movers	_____
	Moving allowance for staff	_____
	Utility/phone hookup	_____

Systems Integration	Consultants	_____
	Hardware	_____
	Software	_____
	Training	_____

Other Costs	Celebration	_____
	New space	_____
	New programs	_____

TOTAL PROJECTED COSTS   _____

Published by the Amherst H. Wilder Foundation   Copyright © 2000 David La Piana

Index

The Wilder Nonprofit Field Guide Series

Dive right in with these shorter books on specific topics

The Wilder Nonprofit Field Guide to:
Conducting Successful Focus Groups

Shows how to collect valuable information without a lot of money or special expertise. Using this proven technique, you'll get essential opinions and feedback to help you check out your assumptions, do better strategic planning, improve services or products, build goodwill, and more.

by Judith Sharken Simon
$15.00   80 pages, softcover   Item# AWF-99-FGC

The Wilder Nonprofit Field Guide to:
Developing Effective Teams

Helps you understand, start, and maintain a team. Provides tools and techniques for writing a mission statement, setting goals, conducting effective meetings, creating ground rules to manage team dynamics, making decisions in teams, creating project plans, and developing team spirit.

by Beth Gilbertsen and Vijit Ramchandani
$15.00   80 pages, softcover   Item# AWF-99-FGD

The Wilder Nonprofit Field Guide to:
Fundraising on the Internet

Your quick road map to using the internet for fundraising. Shows you how to attract new donors, troll for grants, get listed on sites that assist donors, and learn more about the art of fundraising. Includes detailed reviews of 77 web sites useful to fundraisers, including foundations, charities, prospect research sites, and sites that assist donors.

by Gary M. Grobman, Gary B. Grant, and Steve Roller
$15.00   64 pages, softcover   Item# AWF-99-FGF

The Wilder Nonprofit Field Guide to:
Getting Started on the Internet

Learn how to use the internet for everything from finding job candidates to finding solutions to management problems. Includes a list of useful nonprofit sites, and shows you how to use the internet to uncover valuable information and help your nonprofit be more productive.

by Gary M. Grobman & Gary B. Grant
$15.00   64 pages, softcover   Item# AWF-99-FGG

Violence Prevention and Intervention Titles

The Wilder Publishing Center also publishes books on violence prevention and intervention. Below is a listing of our current offerings. To order or get a FREE catalog with more information, please call **1-800-274-6024**. Details on all our publications are also available on our web site at **www.wilder.org**.

The Little Book of Peace

A pocket-size guide to help people think about violence and talk about it with their families and friends. You may download a free copy from our web site at www.wilder.org.

Designed & illustrated by Kelly O. Finnerty
.65 (min. order 10 copies)   24 pages
English version–Item #AWF-97-LBP
Hmong translation–Item #AWF-00-LBH

Journey Beyond Abuse: A Step-by-Step Guide to Facilitating Women's Domestic Abuse Groups

A complete guide for creating a program where women increase their understanding of the dynamics of abuse, feel less alone and isolated, and have a greater awareness of channels to safety.

by Kay-Laurel Fischer, MA, LP & Michael F. McGrane, LICSW
$45.00   208 pages, softcover   Item #AWF-97-JBA

Moving Beyond Abuse

A guided journal for participants. Coordinates with the sessions in *Journey Beyond Abuse*.

$10.00   88 pages, softcover   Item #AWF-97-MBA

Foundations for Violence-Free Living: A Step-by-Step Guide to Facilitating Men's Domestic Abuse Groups

A complete guide to facilitating a men's domestic abuse program. Includes twenty-nine activities, detailed guidelines for presenting each activity, and more.

by David J. Mathews, MA, LICSW
$45.00   240 pages, softcover   Item #AWF-95-FVL

On the Level

Participant's workbook to *Foundations for Violence-Free Living*. Contains forty-nine worksheets where men can record their insights and progress.

$15.00   160 pages, softcover   Item #AWF-95-OTL

What Works in Preventing Rural Violence

An in-depth review of eighty-eight effective strategies to prevent and intervene in violent behaviors. Also includes a Community Report Card to collect, record, and use information about violence in your community.

by Wilder Research Center
$17.00   94 pages, softcover   Item #AWF-95-PRV

Five Easy Ways to Order

Call toll-free: **1-800-274-6024**
Internationally: 651-659-6024

Mail: Amherst H. Wilder Foundation
Publishing Center
919 Lafond Avenue
St. Paul, MN 55104

Fax: 651-642-2061

E-mail: books@wilder.org
On-line: www.wilder.org

Sales tax

Minnesota residents, please add 7% sales tax or attach your tax exempt certificate. FED TAX ID 41-0693889

Shipping & Handling (to each delivery address)

If order totals:	Ground 7-10 business days	Priority 2-3 business days	Next Day Next day by 5:00 pm
Up to $30.00	$4.00	$6.00	$35.00
$30.01 - 60.00	$5.00	$7.00	$40.00
$60.01 - 150.00	$6.00	$8.00	$45.00
$150.01 - 500.00	$8.00	$10.00	$50.00
Over $500.00	3% of order	Call	Call

Priority and Next Day Air orders called or faxed in by 2:00 p.m. EST M-F will be shipped the same day. **Priority and Next Day orders must be prepaid. Outside the U.S. or Canada, add an additional U.S. $5.00.**

Quantity discounts

We offer substantial discounts on orders of ten or more copies of any single title. Please call for details.

www.wilder.org

Want more details? Check out our web site for each book's table of contents, author information, excerpts, and discounts. You can also order on-line.

Order Form

PRICES SUBJECT TO CHANGE

	QTY.	PRICE EACH	TOTAL AMOUNT
Collaboration Handbook: Creating, Sustaining, and Enjoying the Journey		$30.00	
Collaboration: What Makes It Work		15.00	
Community Building: What Makes It Work		20.00	
Consulting with Nonprofits: A Practitioner's Guide		35.00	
Coping with Cutbacks: The Nonprofit Guide to Success When Times Are Tight		20.00	
Marketing Workbook for Nonprofit Organizations Vol. I: Develop the Plan, Revised & Updated		28.00	
Marketing Workbook for Nonprofit Organizations Vol. II: Mobilize People for Marketing Success		28.00	
Pocket Guide for Marketing Representatives (1 copy free with order of Marketing Vol. II)		1.95	
The Nonprofit Mergers Workbook: Considering, Negotiating, and Executing a Merger		28.00	
Resolving Conflict in Nonprofit Organizations		28.00	
Strategic Planning Workbook for Nonprofit Organizations, Revised and Updated		28.00	
The Wilder Nonprofit Field Guide to Conducting Successful Focus Groups		15.00	
The Wilder Nonprofit Field Guide to Developing Effective Teams		15.00	
The Wilder Nonprofit Field Guide to Fundraising on the Internet		15.00	
The Wilder Nonprofit Field Guide to Getting Started on the Internet		15.00	

Send to (please print or attach business card)

Name _____

Organization _____

Address _____

_____

City _____ State _____ ZIP _____

Phone *(in case we have questions)* (_____) _____

We occasionally make our mailing list available to carefully selected companies. If you do not wish to have your name included, please check here ☐

OUR GUARANTEE

If you aren't completely satisfied with any book, simply send it back within 30 days for a full refund.

SUBTOTAL	
7% tax if in MN	
SHIPPING	
TOTAL	

Payment Method

VISA MasterCard AMERICAN EXPRESS Cards

Card # _____

Expiration Date _____

Signature (required) _____

☐ Check/Money Order (payable to A. H. Wilder Foundation)

☐ Bill Me (for orders under $100) PO # _____

Amherst H. Wilder Foundation • Publishing Center • 919 Lafond Ave • St. Paul, MN 55104 • 1-800-274-6024

The Nonprofit Mergers Workbook

Customer Feedback Survey

Dear Reader,

Please take a few moments to give us your feedback. Your responses will help us improve future editions of this book, and will help us improve our service to you. You can either mail the survey to Wilder Publishing Center, 919 Lafond Avenue, St. Paul, MN, USA 55104 or fax it to 651-642-2061. Thank you for your time!

How would you rate this book with regard to its:	Terrible	Poor	OK	Good	Very Good	Out-standing
1. Fit with what you were looking for						
2. Usefulness compared to other materials you've looked at in the same general topic area						
3. Usefulness as a stand alone resource—without the help of a consultant						
4. Organization of information						
5. Value of the worksheets						
6. Overall appearance						
7. Price compared to other books you use in your profession						
8. Amount of time it took to receive your order						
9. Quality of customer service						
10. Condition of the book when it arrived						

11. What is your overall impression of books from the Wilder Foundation?

12. Have you done anything new or different as a result of the information in this publication? If so, what? If not, why not?

13. Is the process outlined in this book easy to follow, or could it be improved?

14. Where do you normally buy or look for books on topics of interest to nonprofit organizations?

15. Do you have any suggestions for books we should develop that would help you in your work?

16. Any other comments?

Your title and organization (optional): _____

THANK YOU! Your comments will help us improve the quality of our publications.